ESSAYS ON THE CHRISTIAN WORLDVIEW AND OTHERS POLITICAL, LITERARY, AND PHILOSOPHICAL

Andrew J. Schatkin

Hamilton Books
A member of
The Rowman & Littlefield Publishing Group
Lanham · Boulder · New York · Toronto · Plymouth, UK

Table of Contents

Preface

In 1969 I graduated from Hunter College of the City of New York with a Bachelors Degree in Greek and Latin, Classical Languages. I studied the ancient languages for four years, having had three years of Latin in high school. I obtained what is presently unobtainable today, a classical education, reading such authors as Homer, Herodotus, Virgil, Catullus, Horace, Propertius, Ovid, and Tibullus, Latin and Greek authors. I even had a course in Latin prose composition, or how to write in Latin.

After I obtained my BA Degree, I was a teacher for a year in the Jesuit High School of Philadelphia, St. Joseph's Preparatory School, teaching Latin. Thereafter, I proceeded to take an M.Div. Degree from Princeton Theological Seminary in Biblical Languages, Greek and Hebrew. I read the entire New Testament in Greek, and much of the Old Testament in Hebrew. As well, I had courses in the Apostolic Fathers, and the Fathers of the Church, St. Augustine and Gregory of Nyssa.

Having obtained my M. Div. Degree, I was then qualified as a lawyer with a J.D. Degree from Villanova Law School. I graduated from Princeton Theological Seminary in 1973 and from Villanova Law School in 1976.

Since then I have been practicing law for over 25 years in the New York Courts, as well as State and Federal courts in other states.

I have had much time to think and reflect having done a great deal of reading and reflection. For better or for worse, I have done a great deal of reading in my life, and I recall at the age of 16 or 17 reading all the works of Charles Dickens one summer vacation. I have had my troubles, trials, and tribulation. I am a believing Christian, committed to the Historical Christian faith. I am a member of the Lutheran Church.

These essays on religion, politics, philosophy, and literature represent a lifetime of reflection and thought. I have thought much, however imperfect my thinking, and however inadequate. I offer these literary, theological, philosophical, and political reflections to the world. I do not fancy myself a great person, and realize my limitations and inadequacies. Nevertheless, I offer these essays in the hope that some person who may chance to read them may find them of interest and help. Perhaps these essays represent my contribution and thought to the faith, once and for all, delivered to the Saints. In these essays, I would hope that the reader will be glorified by the Incarnate Son of God.

I add this. Every writer is indebted to other writers for his thoughts, reflections, and even phrases and ideas: I am particularly indebted for the inspiration in this book to that great Christian Apologist and author, C.S. Lewis. For the essay "Why I Believe in Democracy," I am indebted to the essay entitled "Equality," in the book *Present Concerns* by C.S. Lewis, Harcourt, Inc., 1968. For the essay "The Second Coming of Jesus Christ," I am indebted to C.S. Lewis' essay "The World's Last Night" in his book *The World's Last Night and Other Essays,* Harcourt, Inc., 1987. For the essay "Why I am a Christian," I am indebted to C.S. Lewis' essay "What are we to make of Jesus Christ" in his book *The Grand Miracle,* Valentine Books, 1970. For the essay "Suffering and Pain: A Tentative Answer," I am indebted to C.S. Lewis' book *The Problem of Pain,* HarperOne 2001. For the essay, "Some words about love, or a meditation on love," I am indebted to C.S. Lewis' book *The Four Loves,* Harcourt, Inc., 1991. If there are any other phrases, ideas, or thoughts that I am indebted to from other authors, in particular C.S. Lewis, then my use of those thoughts and reflections is unconscious and imbibed, rather than adopted.

Ad maiorem gloriam Dei.

Chapter 1
Thoughts on a Few Significant Topics

Introduction

In the course of my life, I have formed, as a result of my experiences and content knowledge, certain views about certain things, and I have thought about a few things. I have come to certain conclusions. One, I have determined that the reason why I am a Christian is that there can be no other accounting for the corruption and evil in the world, other than the fall of man into sin, and no other solution than the salvation, forgiveness, and newness of life, and—in a word—eternal life, made available through the grace and salvation of Jesus Christ.

Other religions reject the world and its materiality. Christianity embraces that materiality, says it is good, but says it is imperfect and can be made more perfect in embracing the person and love of Jesus of Nazareth.

Second, as a result of my thinking and experiences in this area, I no longer live for material goods or for culture, or for knowledge, or for intellectual attainment or superiority, but for the love and forgiveness of Jesus Christ. That is the person who I wish to be, and it is in Christ that I live, and not in others or myself.

It follows from that that I must be against abortion, because abortion takes away the human life that God created and made for himself in Christ. Abortion diminishes us all, devalues us all, and makes us all next to nothing. It rewards promiscuity, and says that we are all nothing, worthy of a garbage can. The infinite value that God accords all human beings is so great that for all generations and men, from the beginning of time until the end, he suffered the execution of the cross. How can I not be against abortion, when these are the very persons for whom God sent his only begotten son to be executed as a criminal?

My next idea has some originality. I ask myself why do I believe in democracy? The common fallacy in connection with the democratic system and democracy, is that all men and women are actually equal. I know for a fact that not all of us are equal in talents, abilities, and entertainments. All men and women are equal in the sight of God, in their souls and personhood, and are politically equal in that they are entitled to the same vote. My belief in democracy stems in the fact not that all men are equally good and great, but that all men are equally bad, and because all men are equally bad, no one person or persons can be entrusted with absolute power. Thus, it is the better system, that there be as many majority controls as possible on our elected officials to control human desire and correctitude for power and glory at the expense and stamping down of others, if they can do so. I believe in democracy because I believe that all men given power have a corrupt and blackened heart, and it is better the power be dispersed among as many as possible, rather than be concentrated in the few. That is why I believe in democracy.

Now I come to another set of essays in this book entitled, "Why I Write" and "Why I Read." I write and read because I want to give my imagination free reign and go into other worlds. I want my mind to be expanded beyond its immediate parochial confines into the thoughts and feelings of others, and I want this to be done by the vocalic and beautiful sound of words, both in prose and poetry. I write and read because I want to go beyond myself, into realms of beauty, when otherwise the mundane activity of life eliminates all beauty and goodness in its rush and grayness.

Finally, in this last essay I write about my mother who died in 1999. I have a piercing memory of my mother and her devotion to her husband, to her children, and to her church, and to her Lord. Not a day went by, when I did not see my mother reading the Bible. She wore out three Bibles in the course of her life. I still see her at the piano playing the great hymns of the Protestant Church. I look at her and I look at my own foolish egotism and selfishness and find myself wanting in her life of sacrifice.

I end this introductory section by explaining why I worked for the Legal Aid Society. I worked for the Legal Aid Society, Criminal Defense Division, for seven years, and during that time I dealt with what many would regard as the dregs and garbage of society. Despite their apparent lack of worth in the eyes of the world, I found them worthy and continue to find them worthy. I can only say that God in his infinite wisdom chose the Roman method of execution of a criminal to sacrifice his son for the love of all humanity. It is a paradox that in what is nothing more than an ancient electric chair, the sacrifice of Christ for humanity must find its presence. I worked for the Legal Aid Society, not because I wanted to, but because I had to.

1. Why I Am a Christian

In this age of genetic engineering, extended life spans, riches for some small group of people. and entertainment and possible material enrichment for all, one must ask the question, Why be a Christian? Better put, the question is what we are to make of the claims of Jesus of Nazareth to be God and his claims to show the way to eternal life, conquer death. and offer us, through him, regeneration and a new life, bringing us to a fuller and richer human life. The question, at its outset, is somewhat akin to a fly sitting atop a giraffe and asking what he must do, and it is somewhat absurd, if not comical, in its asking. The question, better put, is what he will make of us, this colossus of history for whom we name our centuries.[1]

Nevertheless, the question is quite pressing. Jesus of Nazareth said things, did things, and made claims that no one else has ever made. He claims to work miracles, feeding five thousand with one fish and one loaf of bread; he claims to change water into wine, cast out whatever demon in our life that may beset us, and he claims to make whole the lame and disabled.

The world tells us to get rich and richer—he tells us to get poor. The secular society tells us to be smart, sophisticated, and in the know—he tells us to be like little children. The world tells us that getting and taking and acquiring is the answer—he tells us that the poor are blessed. The world values dominance, power, and wealth and gives honor and glory to those who obtain its respect—he says the poor in spirit are blessed and the meek will inherit the earth. Media propaganda tells us that everything is getting better and better for everyone—he tells us the world is corrupt and doomed to extinction, to be replaced by a new order.

In a past century of genocides, Armenian, Nazi, Cambodian, Rwandan, and most recently, Darfur, he commands us to love our neighbor as ourselves, telling us that next to the face of God, they are the holiest objects in our affections, destined to be eternal beings.

Jesus of Nazareth consorts and socializes with the outcasts and undesirables, dies the death of an executed criminal, and tells a criminal beside him on the same day that he will be with him in paradise. He says of those that will follow him that they will never die.

No one, before or after, has said the things that he has said, done the things that he has done, and made the fantastic claims that he has made.

In this age of corporate greed, self-love, selfishness, and outright narcissism, he offers a radical alternative to the present secular vision we are told and urged to embrace and believe.

I am a Christian, since I see no other alternative to the corruption, hatred, hostility, and suffering of the present world order based on power, money, and intellectual and material pride. The world tells us to be superior to those around us by whatever method available—he tells us to serve, using our minds, gifts, and talents as a gift of God in the service of others. He makes an exclusive claim. He tells us that class, wealth, race, and sex make no difference.

In a world ruled by greed, egotism, and the desire for dominance, we need a reawakening in the faith of the God of Abraham, Isaac, and Jacob. the God of the majestic theophany of Mount Sinai, the God of the prophets, the God who spoke to Elijah in the still small voice, the God who spoke to Job out of the whirlwind, and the God of the agony at Gethsemane.

For each one of us, he still stands by the waters of the Sea of Galilee bidding rich and poor alike, men and women, peasant and ruler to follow him, and to those who answer and heed his call through the trials, tribulations, suffering, and bittersweet sorrows and joys of this present life, he promises that they will come to know him and who he is, knowing and being known as each one of us truly are, not in our egotism and pride, nor in the flattery of the sycophantic comments of our neighbors and friends.[2]

Finally, as he confronts us at the gates of death, he promises we will reach our full regenerated humanity in and through the faith once and for all delivered to the saints, not the weakened faith of this world in relevance, political correctness, and media jargon, but the faith of Saint Paul, Saint Augustine, Saint Thomas Aquinas, Luther, Calvin, Bonhoeffer, and John Paul II, the faith for which Saint Paul was beheaded by Nero and Saint Peter was crucified upside down before the gates of Rome, and the faith through which and in which we will share eternal knowledge, love, and communion with the source of life, being, and love itself.

2. Why I Am Against Abortion

The right of a woman to so-called reproductive freedom, now established as the law of the land, has become the coded calling card of the modern woman. No longer, the feminist says, are women to be enslaved to the accidents of biology and the mastery of macho men. With this right to so-called reproductive freedom comes, if it did not come before, the right to sexual freedom. The double standard is gone; free and unfettered sexuality is the here and now, since women no longer fear the burden and pain of childbirth and children as a result of the sexual act.

I have been a lawyer for some twenty years at the bar. I go forth as a member of my profession into the 21st century and I feel a pang of guilt that I do not wholeheartedly ascribe and agree with the virtually unbroken insight of some few to date to their right to reproductive freedom and even the idea, as it must follow, that it is the desideratum and the right of all to do exactly what one pleases, either sexually or otherwise, is either desirable or the way to freedom and happiness. This little literary excursus cannot essay to cover all that may be said to be encompassed in the word and notion of freedom: reproductive, sexual, or otherwise. Let it be said and suggested that true freedom lies not in doing what one pleases but in a life of service to others, girded by love and bringing with it, in its train, a lively interest in our fellow human beings, all within the context of the traditional family structure.

What I seek to suggest here is that sexual freedom, the right to choose, or reproductive freedom, the unfettered right to abortion, raises moral questions in my mind and heart and philosophical questions as well. First, simply put, abortion at any age or stage, whether at the inception of pregnancy or in the third trimester, deprives most assuredly and effectively a human, whether defined as potential, in the process of development, or nascent; of her or his chance of life at the least, or a full life at the most.

It is said that it is nothing that should a seedling fall to the ground and it does not grow into a sapling and then a tree, nothing is lost. There are many more seeds that will bear fruit. This evades the issue: that is the value we attach to all human life and ourselves as well. We men and women in our beings have and share dreams, thoughts and loves. We live; we love; we cherish; we reach out everyday in some fashion to all who come our way.

If we ourselves never came into being, then we must say there is no loss. If this states the truth then we must conclude that we ourselves in ourselves and others as well have no value. It is a joy to see the little children at play, but then imagine each little one cut into nothingness and disposed of like excess. It is fine for a woman to be with her newborn abounding in maternal love and affection in the life she has given. It is sad that that very life could well have been cut to death before birth. Unfettered abortion as a right diminishes each one of us, knowing that it could have been you or me and not caring. Unfettered abortion says all of us are nothing. It is beyond religion and it is beyond philosophy. There is something in each of us and in ourselves, however fragmentary and apparently insignificant, that makes each of us something in relation to us all.

My friends and family often ask me why I as a lawyer can at times represent the poor, possibly unkempt and unattractive on the exterior, My answer is that I do not look at the outside and outskirts; not at their economic status, nor their outer attire, but in the soul and heart of the individual.

The right of an unfettered abortion is largely based in our society's emphasis on individual freedom to please one's self at the expense of another. It is based on selfishness and egotism, aiming at some sort of personal fulfillment. If we allow the unborn to die, why not the old and the handicapped, equally burdens on society. The right of a woman or man to free sex is irrelevant. Reproductive and sexual freedoms are guises for devaluation of the person in the name of carnality.

As long as our society continues on its collision course of valuing doing what you want above all, then reproductive freedom is an illusion chaining us to our egotism, selfishness, narcissism and self-love. Reproductive freedom is the ultimate alienation device blinding us to our responsibility to care for others, wherein lies the only freedom there is.

True freedom seeks to connect, not cut off. True freedom of choice is the choice to serve. True freedom values service and care for all. There is nothing free in "freedom." Everything has a price including true freedom. Free abortion is based on promiscuity. It is based on alienation and animalistic behavior, rather than responsibility and caring. Reproductive freedom makes us slaves of our desires, engines of our coldness, walking away from the other to outer darkness.

Perhaps it is the cold calculating choice of ourselves in place of others that may be said to constitute hell, if it exists.

Why am I opposed to abortion: The answer is that when I see the little child in the playground, I see something of myself. I surely value myself. Should I not set the same value on others and not choose to discard another because that other gets in the way of my pleasures.

The right to free choice enslaves us all since it is based on cold hard self-interest in the name of an easy and personal doing what you want. The right to an abortion degrades us all because it says we are all nothing. It is one step to Hell.

Reprinted by permission from Vol. 69, No. 7, April 2006 of the Queens Bar Bulletin.

3. Who I Am and What I Live For

I have now reached the fifth decade of my life. Having worked for some years, thought, read, and occasionally loved, I now approach the question, Who am I and What do I live for? When I was very young I lived to be smart, clever, and more knowledgeable than my contemporaries. I raised Culture and Intellect to the head of virtual gods. I now know that that type of thinking and those goals were entirely and absolutely erroneous.

I would add that for many of us, the goods and goals of life are money and material goods. Moreover, it may be said that many, if not most, of us live our lives for, and in idolization of, ourselves. Most men and women, I would posit, are in a continual and intense process of self-worship and self-love. In short, most of humanity are engaged in a constant and unremitting course of selfishness and self-love, continually convinced of their personal greatness. As I approach, or rather become aware of, my mortality and limited lifespan, I reject these values and ideas as insubstantial and shallow.

I am fortunate in having had an opportunity to spend three years of my life studying the great Christian dogma, ideas, and thinkers. Three particular verses of Holy Scripture define who I am and what I live for. In Revelation 3 :20 Saint John states "Behold, I stand at the door, and knock: if any a man hear my voice, and open the door, I will come into him, and will sup with him, and he with me." The Apostle here states in clear and succinct language that Christ stands at the door of our hearts and souls and bids us not merely to converse with him, but to commune with him. Every human being is faced with the claim of Jesus Christ as he knocks at the door of their hearts and bids that he may enter into and establish relationship with them.

The second verses of Holy Scripture that now define who I am and what I live for are found in Saint Paul's letter to the Roman Church, Chapter 8, verses 38 and 39. In those verses, Saint Paul states, "For I am persuaded, that neither death nor life, nor angels, nor principalities, nor powers, nor things present, nor things to come, nor height, nor depth, nor any other creature, shall be able to separate me from the love of God, which is in Christ Jesus our Lord." The greatest religious thinker in the history of the world does not say that he is smarter than other people; that he is richer than other people; that he is better looking than other people; or that he wishes to be any of those things, but states that nothing in life seen or unseen can separate him from the love of God, which he finds in Jesus Christ.

The third verse of Holy Scripture that also defines who I am is found in St. Paul's letter to the Galatian Christian community, Chapter 3, Verse 28. In that chapter and verse, St. Paul states, "There is neither Jew nor Greek, there is neither slave nor free, there is neither male nor female; for you are all one in Christ Jesus." In one stroke of the pen, St. Paul, the most profound religious thinker in the history of the world, eliminates race, sex, and class divisions.

Who am I and what do I live for?

It is obvious that the world is very evil and very bad, run by forces of dominance, selfishness, self-aggrandizement, a maelstrom of grabbing and getting more and more power and more and more things. The world seeks to keep out the force of the eternal love and mercy of Jesus Christ, which decimates these idols and forces and brings people into love with him and in love with one another. One drop of the love of Jesus Christ can change a continent or a country. The world is hungry for it, but the world system and the forces that define it and govern it seek to exclude that love.

Who am I now and what do I live for?

I live for the undying mercy and love of Jesus Christ, which is the only hope for a broken and twisted humanity and world.

4. Why I Believe in Democracy

A few days ago when I was browsing at a book store in Penn Station, waiting for my Long Island Railroad train, I saw a little book entitled: *The Future of Freedom, Illiberal Democracy at Home and Abroad* by Fareed Zakaria.[3] The book and its contents interested me so I bought the book.

I have no arguments with the author or his publisher and I owe them both good words for the interest and stimulation the book, on cursory examination, afforded me.

Nevertheless, I found the book deeply disturbing even on mere facial examination.

For example, the author in a section entitled, "Problems of Democracy," states that Constitutional liberalism is about the limitation of power; democracy is about its accumulation and use.[4] The author then goes on to state that over the past decade elected governments claiming to represent the people have steadily encroached on the powers and rights of other elements in society.[5]

At another part the author speaks of the tyranny of the majority referencing James Madison and Alexis DeTocqueville. At this juncture the author goes on to state and argue that in many developing countries the experience of democracy over the past few decades has been one in which actual majorities have eroded separations of power, undermined human rights, and corrupted long-standing traditions of tolerance and fairness.[6] Later the author states that the haste to press countries into elections over the last decade has been counterproductive.[7]

In a later section, Mr. Zakaria points out that when Americans are asked what public institutions they most respect, three bodies are always at the top of the list: the Supreme Court, the Armed Forces, and the Federal Reserve System. Mr. Zakaria goes on to state that these three have one thing in common: they are insulated from public pressures and operate undemocratically. Mr. Zakaria then states that Americans admire those institutions precisely because they lead rather than follow. By contrast, Mr. Zakaria states, the Congress, the most representative and reflective of political institutions, stands at the bottom of most surveys.[8]

The author concludes that what we need in politics today is not more democracy, but less. He does say we should not embrace strongmen and dictators, but suggests we should ask why certain institutions in our society such as the Federal Reserve and the Supreme Court function so well and others, such as legislature, fare so poorly.[9]

Mr. Zakaria at another point concludes that modern democracies will face difficult challenges—fighting terrorism, adjusting to globalization, and adapting to an Aging Society—and concludes that those with immense power in our society should embrace their responsibilities, lead and set standards that are not only legal but moral.[10]

I have not read Mr. Zakaria's whole book and hesitate to draw broad conclusions from the excerpts. It would appear Mr. Zakaria seems to suggest that elective representative democracy as government is problematic, unwieldy, and troublesome. He objects to a form of representational legislature, i.e. the Congress, and lauds the Armed Forces and two appointive bodies, the Supreme Court and the Federal Reserve System. He says majority is tyrannical. Mr. Zakaria states we need in our current political system not more democracy, but less and concludes that those with power should lead.

I find these statements and assertions that our system of elective government and political equality are unwieldy and unworkable and should give way to rule by unrepresentative bodies and that those with power should guide the course and that they are uniquely qualified to make the right decisions in this critical time for our nation is an implicit, if not explicit, rejection of our democratic system. I argue here for Democracy and why I believe in this system.

First, as to its defects: Democracy is a system of political equality where those over a certain age are given and may exercise the voting franchise. It is a system of political equality in which all citizens over a certain age are empowered and given the opportunity for political participation.

This has been misinterpreted, or rather extended, to the point that all people in a democratic society are, in fact, actually equal in their talents and abilities. I am and never will be a concert violinist or nuclear physicist, nor an epic poet, or a leading playwright. I do not think I could be a great actor. In sum, a democracy does not imply actual personal equality, since we all differ in whatever gifts we may possess. Democracy is a system of government operating through political equality. At its best democracy provides an equal starting point and some equality of opportunity.

Second, the idea that all are equal leads to a second mistake: In democratic societies there may develop what one may call a "cult of mediocrity." Hence, the desire of most Americans to see in their elected officials and politicians a "regular guy."

This, if one may so call it, "cult of Mediocrity" rejects in a sense any sort of excellence that may distinguish one of us from another; since we are all practically equal we must be actually so in talents, abilities, and attainments. And so it follows that in a democratic system a leveling occurs that results in a kind of adulation of the average and mediocre.

This is the second failing, if it can be called so, of a democratic system, or it can be.

Yet, all in all, I fully believe in a democratic system of government in which the officials who govern us, our leaders as it were, are subject to the scrutiny of the voting electorate.

I do not believe in democracy as merely a form of government because people are actually equal, since that is not true. I believe in democracy, well knowing that power, if concentrated in the few or in one person, will be abused. Power given to one or a few will be abused because on some deeper level there exists an innate corruption in human nature that cannot be evaded, escaped, or eradicated. Whether the abuse occurs in the context of a traditional marriage where one economically dependent spouse is subject to the untrammeled authority of the other or resides in a CEO with unlimited power over the lives and livelihood of his employees, that power will be abused.

I believe in Democracy because men, if given the chance, are so bad that no man alone can be entrusted with unchecked power over his fellows. I oppose slavery because I fear and oppose Masters. Men, given the chance, will allow their egotism, selfishness and desire to dominate and to rule. The baseness and corruption of their hearts, given the chance, will come to full flower.

Democracy posts that men, far from being equal, are always prone to the blackguard. Democracy distributes and checks power, doing so by a process of elective accountability and a system of check and balances.

I believe in Democracy not because men are good or because everyone is the same or because everyone is equal Democracy may not be the best and most effective form of government, but it is the only alternative, since it recognizes that the rule of the elite, few or appointed will and must be subject to the control of the electorate, not because those few are especially and particularly evil or bad—and the majority are not—but because without controls, rules or limits they can and will be so.

We have laws to control untrammeled, human nature. Without them we are barbarians. Unlimited power in one or few, uncontrolled and unaccounted for, will and must give way to the blackheartedness that resides only slightly beneath the surface of us all.

Democracy envisions not a world of total good and perfection but a world that requires a wide dispersal of control and power in as many as possible, knowing who we are as human beings and what we may actually do.

This article is reprinted from Vol. 68, No. 5, Feb. 2005 of the Queens Bar Bulletin *by permission.*

5. *Why I Write*

I often ask myself, why do I write? Writing is labor; it is lonely and isolated. I have, thus far, gained from this labored servitude, no fame and little money. In short, writing is hard work sometimes, with little or no possibility of reward or rewards in sight.

I here offer some reasons for "Why I Write." First, I love and enjoy what may be called the vocalic sounds of words. Words, as more than a medium of bare boned communication, express in and through themselves many qualities of near poetic beauty. Words can express the deepest and most profound of religious feeling and insight; the most beautiful vision and apprehension of nature; the depths of romantic love; and the most profound of philosophical ideas and thinking.

Words can be put to use in the casual and informal essay, as well as the long narratives and conventions of the novel as it has developed for the past 500 years. Words can express through alliteration, assonance, rhythm and rhyme, sounds and forms that bring us to the face of their own particular beauty.

In sum, I write because I enjoy the sounds of words.

Second, I write because I enjoy expressing my thoughts in a coherent form.

Thoughts only orally expressed, first are impermanent and second undeveloped. The developed written word allows the expression of coherent thinking, whereby ideas and concepts and thoughts can be made permanent and expressed to a wider and wider audience.

Third, I think I write because I wish to have a place in the stream of history, where other minds will, perhaps, remember me and think of me, and my thoughts and ideas, when I am long gone. I write because I have the selfish and egotistical desire to have a place in the stream of future generations. I wish, in an act of egotism, to have a place in the pantheon, a comer in the arena of history.

Thus, I write, not only because I enjoy to express my thoughts and ideas in the most elegant and literary way I can, but also because I wish a place in the stream of history.

Fourth, I also write because I think I have something to say. I am not so dominant and self-involved that I think my thoughts are entirely original, since many of them come from the reading of the major writers and thinkers I have done in the course of my lifetime. But I do think, in some little way, that I can, so to speak, contribute my little widow's mite through my writing and offer the world something of value and interest. Simply, I write because I have something to say that I think and believe people might be interested in.

The sacrifice involved in the task of writing is great and daunting, but I still think, even with the dominance of visual image and sound communication, that writing will always, properly used, be able to express the loftiest, most profound, deepest, and most beautiful ideas and apprehensions that the human mind can express.

6. Why I Read

We live in a time of the visual and sound. Day in and day out we are all assaulted by images and blaring sound, whether cable television, movies, DVDs, or the internet. The world moves faster and faster. It would appear that print, as a form of mass communication, is, if not fast disappearing, then on the wane.

Many people read only if compelled to do so to gain fast and immediate information. The very concept of literature and books is in danger of extinction. One must ask, why read?

The question is a pressing one, since books and literature, as modes of pleasure and intellectual stimulation, are in peril.

It must be said, as a matter of clear thinking, that there is not greater intrinsic value to be attached to print, as opposed to sound and image.

If vision and sound may be said to equally inform and entertain as printed books, they are not to be criticized or decried.

Yet, all in all, I continue to read, and I offer two reasons. First, books and literature take me to regions of thinking and imagination that I would otherwise be deprived of. Milton in *Paradise Lost* takes me to the fall of man from paradise. Homer takes me to the epic warrior culture. Dante takes me to the worldview of the Middle Ages, if not the Christian worldview of Paradise, Purgatory, and the Inferno. Anthony Trollope takes me to the world of the Victorian landed aristocracy and the clergy of the Church of England. Each great work of literature and author offers me distinct and different imaginative pleasures.

Second, these pleasures, as they are offered, are not quick and fleeting. They engage, stretch and involve my mind and spirit. They open new vistas to me and offer me new directions.

Every great work of literature, whether philosophy, poetry, or the novel, offer me peculiar pleasures, not in a fleeting image or thunderous sound, where we are mere passive recipients, but in a process of involvement and development.

I read because, in truth, I enter other realms and other minds and I gain access in a profound and lasting way to idea, concepts, insights, and values I would otherwise be cut off from and be in intellectual deprivation of.

Every great work of literature expands my being and brings me into the minds, souls, and imagination of others. I remain myself, yet share what these minds may give me or offer me.

Reading for me is an adventure, taking me to places and realms I would never have been, and taking me to regions of imagination I might never know. Sitcoms cannot replace Keats, nor *Leave It To Beaver* offer competition to *War and Peace*. The first is a quick fix; the others offer a level of involvement and learning that stretches our souls and minds beyond the superficial offerings of television and movies. The one offers imaginative involvement, and in the other we remain, at best, passive recipients of superficiality.

7. *My Mother: A Memory*

On December 12, 1999, my mother died. She had been ill for a long time: falls; a broken leg; a broken shoulder; the loss of vision in one eye; a cataract in the other.

She was in Boston, Massachusetts when the end came. She had come there from her home in New York in 1994 when, after two falls, two hospitalizations, and two recuperative periods, she could no longer, in her words "do it" as wife of my father who was elderly and ailed, and as mother of three grown children whom she never failed to have for "Sunday dinner," until her body would no longer allow her to do so. In 1994, she was forced to leave the home in which I and my two sisters had grown from childhood to adolescence and then to adulthood.

After a year of refusing to get out of bed and refusing to eat, she was hospitalized in Massachusetts General with an infection that would not leave her and pulled her down so that one night at age 84 her heart stopped. Thus, this devoted wife and mother, whose life was a gift of love in the service of others, ceased to be.

When I heard the news over the phone from my sister, I felt the loss with a sense of relief that it was over and that I was free of childhood bonds and attachments.

Little did I know my loss.

From my earliest years, I see my mother reading. At first, I did not know what she read, but I did know that somehow I wanted to be like that: a lover of literature. Later, I came to know, very early, that not a day passed in which she did not read the King James Version of the English Bible. In her daily reading, often at night, she wore out three bibles.

One summer, she told me she was reading all of Dickens. Another year she read all of Calvin's *Institutes of the Christian Religion.* Now, I see my mother at the piano playing her favorite German Lieder and playing and singing the great hymns of the Protestant Church. No Sunday passed when she did not attend church.

My mother lived and loved music and literature. She knew Latin; spoke fluent Spanish; was well read in German poetry; and then, when my sister studied ancient Greek in college, she studied with her at home.

My mother loved the church and loved Jesus of Nazareth. She loved music and literature as an expression of her love for God and Christ.

Withal, despite her education and humanistic values she lived a life of giving, not taking; loving, not grasping; always doing the humble work of a wife and mother and never asking or seeking recompose. She spent her short time on earth for her church, her husband and her children.

I have her no longer, but not a day or hour passes when I do not think of her love, her compassion, her selflessness, and her devotion to what makes us a little more human than we thought we could possibly be.

I compare my egotism, selfishness and worldly lust for greed and power with her life and sacrifice. I find myself wanting, yet I know that I still see her face and her bright eyes, even in death, granting me her forgiveness and excusing my stupidity.

8. *Why I Work for the Legal Aid Society*

I work for the Legal Aid Society, Criminal Defense Division. Daily I wend my way through the Criminal Courts of the Borough of Queens on behalf of indigent defendants charged with the most horrendous crimes: Rape, Attempted Murder, Sale and Possession of Drugs. All these are the meat and drink of my day. My clients are poor and helpless. They are the societal underclass, mostly black and Hispanic. Many will plead guilty to a lesser criminal charge, fearful of the consequences of trial if found guilty. It seems that I am fighting a losing battle as an advocate of the poor. The District Attorney, as advocate of the People of the State of New York, is against me and sometimes it seems that the Judge is not my friend. Yet I persevere with a will.

My parents, my friends, my acquaintances ask me—why do you represent this "guilty" underclass? Why be the lawyer and friend to these suckers on the wheal of society, these men and women who think nothing of robbing, pillaging, and destroying the property and person of their neighbors and fellow citizens of the commonwealth?

Sometimes the answer is not easy to give. Certainly, I gain no substantial financial reward for my efforts. I am lucky if the public, my friends and even my family tolerate or even respect my commitment. My sister, a University Professor of Music, has often said to me she would much prefer if I were a prosecutor sending the "guilty" to jail and so ridding society, for a time, of these bloodsuckers and destroyers of temporal peace and tranquility.

My uncle, a Doctor, who phones me often, asks me how I can let a seemingly guilty client go free on a legal technicality. A Sixth Grader in Nassau County elementary school asked me, after I had spoken to the class on my work as a defense lawyer, if I would actually represent a client whom I knew for a fact was guilty?

The answer to all these questions is not easy for the comfortable middle class man or woman secure financially and privileged with a job, personal, and financial security, who has never been homeless, never without a skill and never without a job or the secure emotional backing of a loving family.

Yet, I gladly represent the poor and accused, knowing first that I have been given so much and they have so little. Poverty, ignorance, and unhappiness are the lot of these societal victims. They are the last to be hired at the lowest wages and the first to be fired. They live in a background of fathers who have fled family support obligations, alcoholism, sexual promiscuity and drug abuse. They are the high school dropouts who look for work and cannot find it, and then drift to the streets. They are the ones society has left behind and forgotten. Yet, somehow they are terribly important. Should we abandon and should I abandon the defense of the poor, albeit criminally accused, I diminish myself as a man and our free society lessens itself.

The day you or I or any man or woman turns his back on the vilest and poorest we are men without chests and women without hearts. It is in all of the religions, all of the faiths: Judaism, Islam, Buddhism, Confucianism, and Christianity. Our duty to the poorest and most baseless is all the greater. It is all the same. It is the way of civilized man, to support the widows, orphans and poor in their need and affliction. Justice and mercy demand no more and no less. The time that we as a society and I as a Member of the Bar turn our backs on the defense of the vilest, poorest and most reprehensible of the criminally accused, we abandon not only our obvious constitutional responsibilities as citizens of a free and democratic society, but our moral and ethical responsibilities as feeling, loving, and fully human persons.

No man or woman is an island. We are all part of the Main. "Every man's death diminishes me." So said John Donne the 17th Century poet.

The day I abandon the poorest, the most indefensible is the day I become less than a man and less than a lawyer. It is only the poor who sleep in the subways. It is only the mentally ill who sleep in the streets. It is only the jobless who drift on the city pavement. I defend the indigent criminally accused not because I want to but because I have to. The corporations and companies have their counsel. I choose to defend not in the tradition of fees but of human and societal justice to represent the poor. Let our city be on note that the day I or my brothers and sisters of the bar abandon this responsibility is the day of reckoning for us all.

Reprinted from The Summation, *the newsletter of the of the Criminal Courts Bar Association of Queens County, January 1992.*

Notes

1. C.S. Lewis, "What do we make of Jesus Christ," in *The Grand Miracle and other Selected Essays on Theology and Ethics from God and the Dock* (New York: Random House, 1970), 111.

2. Albert Schweitzer, *The Quest of the Historical Jesus* (Baltimore, Md.: The Johns Hopkins University Press, 1998), 403.

3. Fareed Zakaria, *The Future of Freedom* (New York: WW. Norton, 2004).

4. Zakaria, *The Future of Freedom*, 101-102.

5. Zakaria, *The Future of Freedom*, 102.

6. Zakaria, *The Future of Freedom*, 106.

7. Zakaria, *The Future of Freedom*, 155.

8. Zakaria, *The Future of Freedom*, 241.

9. Zakaria, *The Future of Freedom*, 248.

10. Zakaria, *The Future of Freedom*, 256.

Chapter 2
The Christian Worldview

Introduction

The Christian worldview has become somewhat foreign to the secular world, since it assumes a world tripartite in character. Above all is God in his Heaven, in the company of angels; below that is the world and the universe, inhabited by men, women, and animals; and finally there is Hades or Hell, the province of the fallen angels and Lucifer, the rebellious angel. This is only part of the Christian worldview. I have given some consideration and thought to what constitutes the Christian worldview, and some of these essays will attempt to present what I believe to be the Christian worldview on certain discrete and set topics.

First, I have often thought about why the Psalms, the manna of the Church, contain hostility, malice, and curses. In this first essay, I consider various passages from the Psalms, illustrating these cursings, if not hatred and malice, which are at variance with God's love in Christ for all men, and I offer some explanations. When the Psalmist speaks of his enemies, he mirrors our experiences in the world today, whether in Darfur or Iraq. Second, many of these psalms are ascribed to King David, who had many enemies and was persecuted. Third, God, who is love, abhors sin; his holiness cannot abide it. Hence, the malice, hatred and cursings in the Psalms.

Then I speak of the Second Coming of Christ. The Christian community, after the death, resurrection, and ascension of Christ into heaven, imminently expected Christ to return. This essay speculates how this may be and how it will be. Christ will not appear in humility, but in glory. We will all be judged and revealed as who we are as persons. Finally, the Second Coming of Christ will be a final event; the old corrupt world will pass, and a new regenerated world will replace it.

In the next essay entitled, "The Riddle of Jesus Christ," I go through the Gospel of Matthew and point out the contradictions and characteristics of Jesus. I point out the outrageous and insane claim of Jesus to be God and the way to God. It is in the person of Christ that we will all be found and made whole as persons.

The next two essays entitled, "The Idea of a Christian Society" and "The Measure of God's Love," examine what I think may constitute the Christian society, and I conclude that it will include the traditional family, along with a society somewhat socialistic, rather than capitalistic, in its set up. Following this, the essay, "The Measure of God's Love" speaks of infinite love of God, whose magnitude cannot be understood, other than we know that Christ died for all men and women who have ever lived, whom he never knew. We human beings would certainly not be willing to die for those we love, let alone for those we do not know, are indifferent to, do not care about, and do not like or love.

The essays, "Is Poverty Blessed?" and "A Few False Idols," consider the question why Jesus rejects wealth as the answer to our ills. I conclude that material wealth presents a barrier to faith, belief, and spirituality, and is in some sense a barrier to personal growth, since with great material wealth, we come to believe we are somehow autonomous and invincible. The essay, "A Few False Idols," examines how people may pin their sense of self importance. For some, it is material goods; for others they may say they are smarter and more educated or better cultured; some say because they have greater physical strength they are able to dominate their environment; for another group it is looks; and some believe they are morally superior because of their great religious faith. This method, I posit in this essay, of pinning our hopes on what we fancy is some superior quality attached to ourselves lacks truth. For the true believing Christians, all souls and all people have value.

The next literary excursus in this section is an essay on love. In this essay I consider the never ending and unceasing search for love by everyone and all. I define the various forms of love, including romantic love; erotic love; friendship; the love of a parent for a child; love of siblings; the love for animals; the love of nature; and the overwhelming love of God for all mankind. I conclude that all these loves come crashing at the end of our lives and are taken from us and destroyed by death. For the Christian, however, our destruction and death by God's act of love in Christ makes us new men and new women in a new world.

I then speak of "Hell and Damnation." This is an uncomfortable topic in the modern world, but unfortunately it has the support of Holy Scripture and the words of Christ, and is fully articulated in the Creeds of the Church and in its doctrine. I suggest in this essay that we make our own way to hell in our lives and walk there ourselves. What we make of our lives in this life results in heaven or hell in the next. If we are uncharitable, unkind, unforgiving, ungiving, malicious, hard on others, and engulfed in ourselves, we will spend the rest of our lives with whatever we have made of ourselves with those qualities attached to us.

"Who Reads the Bible and Why" is my next topic. I define three types of Bible readers or nonreaders. First, those who neither know, nor care; second, those who regard it as an ancient literary document of intellectual and artistic interest; and third, those who resort to it and read it for guidance and understanding of the ultimate things and moral guidance in this life. I suggest to you that the third category of readers is the only effectual and true understanders of Holy Scripture.

I speak next in this book of "Whatever Happened to Sin and Evil." In the modern world, there is a disinclination and rejection of the existence of sin and evil. With the onset of psychiatry and excuses for human failing founded in genetics and environment, the reality of evil and sin has been downplayed, if not eliminated, and surely is rarely discussed or ever spoken about. The fact of the matter is that wrongdoing, evil, and to use that old word "sin", are very pressing realities and always will be. Whether they emerge in a fractious marriage, an unremitting employer, a sadistic criminal, or anyone who abuses power, including the heads of state, sin and evil has to be admitted and cannot be talked away. Human nature is crooked, defective, twisted, and corrupt. To say this is not so is to ignore history, which is replete with wars, brute force, inhumanity, and sadism. The fact of the matter is, despite the modern world's soft whispers behind a curtain concerning evil, we execute and punish wrongdoers for their misdeeds, thereby recognizing the ever-present reality of wrongdoing and wickedness.

My next essay speaks of "Prayer." I suggest that prayer is not an exercise in formality, but it is an attempt for the child to converse with its parent and have a relationship. Prayer is conversation and relationship. It is an attempt by human beings to relate to the love of their Creator, and attach themselves to that love.

Next I speak of "Suffering and Pain" and I attempt to offer an answer. I speak first of natural pain; this comes to us from disease, illness, and natural disasters. I then go on to speak of the pain inflicted by others. I suggest in this essay that pain exists because without pain and suffering we will cease to grow as human beings and develop compassion for those around us and their suffering and tribulations. Next, I speak of Christ who took pain and suffering upon himself for the love of humanity. We cannot follow Christ without following and attaching ourselves, on some level, to his pain, sacrifice, and suffering. I conclude that pain comes out of our degraded and corrupt human nature, coming out of a fallen world, and when we take on pain, we, on some level, become more fully human, enabling us to overcome our selfishness and self-love.

The next essay in this section of this book, considers the issue of "Priests or Priestesses." I say that the person who celebrates the Eucharist, or to use the Protestant terminology communion, stands in the place instead of Christ, and in that sense it is inappropriate and unfitting for a woman to take on that particular role.

In the next essay I talk about "The Two Christmases." The true Christmas has to do with the entrance of God into history through his only begotten son, Jesus Christ. The modern secular Christmas, has no connection with the true Christmas and is some generalized time of good will in which gifts are exchanged and in which money is made, as a result, by the commercial sector of society.

To go on, in the next little essay in this book entitled, "The Christian Worldview," I posit that the Christian worldview discusses the fall of man into sin; human purpose as created to exist and commune with his Father and Creator; God's covenant with the Jewish people; the rebellion of Lucifer brought about by his overweening pride, refusal to serve, and desire for total independence and autonomy; the Bible as the revealed word of God; and Jesus Christ as the only way that we can come to know and understand God. This introduction, however, does not fully understand the content of this essay, but is a bit of a glimpse into my thoughts.

The next essay in this book is about, "Forgiveness.". Forgiveness is a bit of an irony and conundrum, since our natural inclination is to strike back or, better put, return the favor to those who hurt us. Forgiveness is not excusing or ignoring, but returning the pain inflicted us with love and understanding. It is not forgetting, but responding with love.

The next two essays in this book speak of "Salvation and Sacrifice" and "The One Way to God." As to the second essay, "The One Way to God," I maintain that the only way that we can truly know God is through his only begotten son, Jesus Christ who, with love that we cannot understand and comprehend, died for all men and all generations that have ever lived and that will ever live, dying for those who are indifferent to him, hate him, ignore him, and pay no attention to him. "Salvation and Sacrifice" posits that the need for salvation is due to our fallen, degraded and corrupt human nature, and that the sacrifice of Christ on the cross was God's method of rescuing humanity from death and annihilation.

The next essay speaks of "The Compassion of Christ." Any thinking person who reads the Bible, and especially the New Testament, is struck by the compassion of Christ. His contemporaries did not understand or comprehend why a literate rabbi would consort with publicans and sinners. The criticism made of Jesus in his time was how any responsible, respectable person could consort with the persons, in their time, regarded as low lifes. Obviously, Jesus saw things differently, and it was his compassion that led him to heal, help, forgive, and ultimately take the slow and painful road to suicide and execution.

In the next essay I speak of the "Image of God in Man." I speak and discuss that Jesus in his life was the image of God that leads us to an understanding of God's nature.

In the next two essays, "The Idea of the Supernatural" and "Freedom vs. Slavery," I discuss the modern world's rejection of the supernatural and explain that it is misleading to depend solely on materialism as an anchor and under-

standing of existence. In the essay "Freedom vs. Slavery" I suggest that true
freedom is love and service to others and that slavery is self-love and selfishness.

"Creeds or Chaos" and "Orthodoxy" discuss that the Christian faith is not
merely a matter of some generalized niceness or kindness, but has a dogmatic
structure that cannot be escaped.

Finally, in the essays about evolution and intellect, I first suggest that the
theory of evolution is wanting in reasonableness and intellectual validity since it
is only common sense to observe that everything has a cause, and that fish do
not suddenly become mammals, and primates do not suddenly become men,
however long the passage of time. In the final essay in this group, on what constitutes intelligence or being smart, I say that the modern world places too great
an emphasis on smartness and intellect, or IQ, and does so since that is how we
get on in our lives and raise ourselves economically and personally. This is a
development from the prior method of crude and brute force, or better put, taking and getting by muscle and aggressiveness alone. I conclude that for the
Christian, charity or love, as St. Paul speaks of it in his thirteenth chapter to the
church in Corinth, is true intellect, as opposed to the superficial smartness and
quickness that our modern age tells us to have.

1. Hostility and Malice in the Psalms

The Bible is a very old and ancient book. The Psalms are also a very old book
and stem from antiquity. How old we do not know precisely. This much can be
said: that when we read the Psalms, or rather listen to them, as we should listen
to lyric poetry, we look down the throat of antiquity. We hear and see homicidal,
manic Hebrews dancing and singing before the temple, a place of animal sacrifice. We do not know how old the Psalms actually are, nor do we know who the
author is, although tradition has ascribed them to King David.

Psalms 72 and 110 have been traced to persons and events in the Hellenistic
Age; Psalm 46 has been connected with the raising of the Assyrian siege of Jerusalem in 701 B.C.; and Psalm 74 has been connected to the fall of Jerusalem
in 586 B.C.[1]

The Psalms were probably written by many poets, at different times. C.S.
Lewis in his *Reflections on the Psalms*[2] stated that Psalm 18 may be from David
himself.

The Psalms are lyric poetry and many of them may be denominated as
hymns. One of the most distressing motifs, or subjects or expressions, throughout the Psalms is the constant reiteration and repetition of hostility and malice.[3]
Let me add that my knowledge of Hebrew is amateurish, and I approach this
subject lacking in expert knowledge and with the perspective of a novice.

Let us take a walk through the Psalms and examine this reiterated expression of malice and hostility, mainly directed towards the Psalmist's "enemies." In Psalm 2, verse 9, the Psalmist states of the heathen, that the Lord will "bruise them with a rod of iron: and break them in pieces like a potter's vessel." In Psalm 5, verse 6, it states of the foolish that "thou shalt destroy them and speak leasing: the Lord will abhor both the bloodthirsty and deceitful man." In Psalm 6, verse 10, the poet says that his enemies will be confounded, vexed, turned back, and put to shame suddenly. In Psalm 7, verses 13 and 14, the writer says that if a man will not turn, the Lord will whet his sword, and in verse 14, the writer goes on to say that God has prepared for this man, the instruments of death. In Psalm 9, the poet states of his enemy that "destructions are come to a perpetual end: even as the cities, which thou has destroyed, their memorial is perished with them." In verse 17 of that same Psalm, the poet says, "that the wicked should be turned into hell: and all people that forget God."

In Psalm 11, verse 7, the poet says of the Lord that "upon the ungodly he shall rain snares, fire, and brimstone, storm in tempest: this shall be their portion to drink." In Psalm 18, verse 37, the Psalmist says that he, "will follow upon mine enemies and overtake them: and neither will I turn again till I have destroyed them." In verse 38, the poet says of his enemies, "I will smite them, that they shall not be able to stand: but fall under my feet." In verse 39, the poet says of his enemies, "thou shalt throw down mine enemies under me", and in verse 40 "thou has made mine enemies to also turn their backs upon me: and I shall destroy them that hate me." In verse 42, the poet concludes of his enemies, "I will beat them as small as the dust before the wind: I will cast them out as the clay in the streets." In Psalm 21, verses 8-10, the Psalmist says of his enemies,

> All thine enemies shall feel thine hand:
>   thy right hand shall find out them that hate thee.
> Thou shalt make them like a fiery oven
>   in time of thy wrath
> the Lord shall destroy them in his displeasure,
>   and the fire shall consume them.
> Their fruit shall thou root out of the earth:
>   and their seed from among the child of men.

Psalm 23 is one of the most familiar and beautiful of the Psalms.[4] In the midst of these beautiful lyrics that present a picture motif of the Lord feeding and walking the believer and righteous man through the valley of the shadow of death, the Psalmist says that he exalts in having a feast prepared on his behalf before and in the presence of his enemies. The exaltation in personal vengeance, on the part of the poet, stands out in the midst of this most beautiful of lyric poems. He is happy; while his enemies look on, he feasts and takes his pleasures in and before them.

In Psalm 41, verse 8, the poet states of his enemies, "let the sentence of guiltiness proceed against him: and now that he lieth let him rise up no more." In Psalm 35, verses 1-8, the Psalmist says of his enemies,

Plead thou my cause, O Lord, with them that strive with me:
    and fight thou against them that fight against me.
Lay hand upon the shield and buckler:
    and stand up to help me.
Bring forth the spear, and stop the way
    against them that persecute me:
Say unto my soul,
    I am thy salvation.
Let them be confounded and put to shame,
    that seek after my soul:
Let them be turned back and brought to confusion,
    that imagine mischief for me.
Let them be as the dust before the wind:
    and the angel of the Lord scattering them.
Let their way be dark and slippery:
    and let the angel of the Lord persecute them.
For they have privily laid their net to destroy me without a cause:
    yea, even without a cause have they made a pit for my soul.
Let a sudden destruction come upon him unawares,
    and his net, that he hath laid privily, catch himself:
    that he may fall into his own mischief.

In Psalm 55, verse 16, the poet writes of his enemies, "let death come hastely upon them, and let them go down quick into hell." In Psalm 83, verses 13-17, the Psalmist says of his enemies:

O my God, make them like unto a wheel:
    and as the stubble before the wind;
Like as the fire that burneth up the wood:
    and as the flame that consumeth the mountains.
Persecute them even so with thy tempest:
    and make them afraid with thy storm.
Make their faces ashamed, O Lord:
    that they may seek thy Name.
Let them be confounded and vexed ever more and more:
    let them be put to shame, and perish."

In Psalm 56, verse 9, the Psalmist says of his enemies that they be put to flight. In Psalm 69, verses 22 through 29, the Psalmist states of his enemies,

Let their table be made a snare to take themselves withal:
    and let the things that should have been for their wealth be unto them an
    occasion of falling.

Let their eyes be blinded, that they see not:
    and ever bow thou down their backs.
Pour out thine indignation upon them:
    and let thy wrathful displeasure take hold of them.
Let their habitation be void:
    and no man to dwell in their tents.
For they persecute him whom thou has smitten:
    and they talk how they may vex them whom thou has wounded.

In Psalm 92, verse 8, the writer states of his enemies that they shall perish and all workers of wickedness shall be destroyed. Psalm 109 is the most distressing and perplexing of the malice and hatred reflected in the Psalms I have just referred to. The Psalmist in verse 6 says that his prayers should be turned into sin, in verse 7 he states that he wishes that his days be few, in verse 8 he states that he wishes his children to be fatherless and his wife a widow, in verse 9 he wishes for his enemies' children to be vagabonds and beg their bread, in verse 10 he wishes that the extortionist consume all that he have, in verse 11 he says that there should be no man to pity him or have compassion for his fatherless children, in verse 12 the poet wishes that his posterity be destroyed and in the next generation his name be put out cleanly. Finally, in verse 13, he says that the sin of his enemy's mother be not done away with, and that the wickedness of his fathers be had in remembrance in the sight of the Lord and in verse 14, the poet says and wishes of his enemies that the Lord may root out the memorial of them from off the earth.

The hostility, hatred, and malice expressed in this hymn and lyric poem, which comes under the rubric of sacred poetry, is astounding, shocking, and to the casual and modern reader is beyond comprehension.[5]

In Psalm 110, the writer says that he wishes that the Lord make his enemies God's footstool. In Psalm 132, the writer states in verse 19 that as for his enemies, "I shall clothe them in shame." In Psalm 140, verses 9 and 10, the poet says and wishes of his enemies, "Let burning coals fall upon them, let them be cast into the fire and into the pit, that they never rise up again."

Analysis and Conclusion

This brief overview of the motif of wishing the worst upon those whom the poet feels persecute and hurt him is perplexing to the believing Christian or any decent person, whether religious or otherwise. How can we explain, in the Bible which constitutes the revelation of God's love in Christ, this vitriolic hatred? How did this hate, temper, and hostility find its way into the most sacred of books? I offer two, if not speculative, thoughts and conclusions.

First, the world is no different than it was in 750 B.C. It is a place of struggle, dominance, power, egotism, selfishness, and hate. The world is a place in which love has little or no place. It is a place of survival; it is the beast in the jungle; it is making one's way through a hostile morass. When the Psalmist speaks of his enemies and wishes them as ill as he can, he speaks of those who even today conspire against others to damage, hurt, and devour them. The poet's experience in the depths of antiquity mirror our experiences in the world today, whether in Bosnia, Nazi Germany, Darfur, or Iraq.

Second, I offer another theory or explanation. Many of these Psalms are ascribed to King David who had many enemies and was persecuted by many. Thus, these cursings upon enemies may be ascribed, possibly, to events in King David's life.

Third, I offer another view and perspective. God, who is love, abhors sin and wickedness. He does not hate the individual sinner, but hates malice, negativity, taking, destroying, and seeking to get the better of others to enrich and gain ground for oneself. This hatred of sin is reflected in the hostility and malice which is so perplexing in the Psalms. One cannot understand Psalm 109, which wishes so much harm upon the ungodly sinner, without understanding that God, who is light, goodness and holiness, abhors sin and its horrible manifestations.

2. The Second Coming of Jesus Christ

The doctrine or dogma of the return, or second coming, of Christ is little emphasized or mentioned in the Church today. It is, in fact, part of the Christian dogmatic and belief system. The early Christians imminently expected Christ to return and establish his Kingdom. Our Lord himself said that he would return, however late or soon. The Doctrine is distinctly and specifically stated in the Apostles Creed.

Conservative Protestant Fundamentalists emphasize the Doctrine, saying that the end of the world is coming soon, along with the return and second coming of Christ. Some, in the past, have sought and essayed to fix and predict the date of Christ's return, and have been sadly disappointed.

What are we to say of this particular manifestation of the Christian faith?

First, we are told that we do not know when it will occur, that we must be always ready. Our Lord says that he will come as a thief in the night. When he comes, he will come to us unawares, perhaps as we are about to marry; write that great novel, take that luxurious vacation, or get that wonderful raise or promotion. All that will end and shrink to insignificance.

We are the actors in this play. We do not know the drama or the script, its beginning, end, or outcome. Only the author knows.

Only the eternal God and the company of Heaven know the story, our role, and the meaning of everything.

Second, Christ will return, not as he came the first time in humility and poverty, but as a ruler of the world and the universe itself. He will not come as a humble carpenter, but as an awesome ruler, to whom all humanity will submit and before whom be brought to their knees. Their submission will not be forced as the world rules by force and wealth, but by the realization of their self-knowledge made known to them by the power and rule of his love. All of us, and each of us, will finally and completely know and be known. There will be no escape. Whoever and whatever we are will be revealed to us and to everyone around us. Neither our wealth, our worldly position in society, our race, our sex, our clothes, our car, our intelligence, nor education will hide who we are. There will be no hypocrisy and no dissimulation. Only the truth about each of us will be known, whether our pride, our false humility, our faking, or, in short, our lies about ourselves that we give to the world during our lives.

Third, the return of Christ will be a final event. It will be the end of everything, and a new beginning. All we thought, said, or planned will be replaced, if not destroyed.

As much as death is final, so the return of Christ, the second coming will be a final event. The curtain will be rung down, the play ended, and everything about all of us will be revealed and made known. The finality of death will end its rule to be taken over by the final eternal rule of the Savior, Redeemer, and Judge of all mankind, a rule, power, and kingdom that will end the corruption, inequality, baseness, pain, and suffering of a world dominated by malice, hatred, and evil, and giving in its place a universe of beauty, goodness, purity, truth, and love, a new and regenerated world of infinite intellectual growth, infinite love, and infinite relationships, where we are no longer bound by our broken and twisted humanity, but stand astride the universe itself, in relationship with its Creator and Redeemer, the source of all life and being.[6]

3. The Riddle of Jesus Christ

Who Jesus Christ, or rather Jesus of Nazareth, was is a question that has fascinated and teased men and women from the time of his death to present day. Albert Schweitzer wrote an important book entitled *The Quest of the Historical Jesus* in which he attempted to outline the history of criticism and research as to who Jesus was, or rather who Schweitzer thought he really was. For believing Christians, Jesus Christ is the son of God who died for all mankind, offers them eternal life if they believe in him, reigns in Heaven, and promises to return to establish a new world and cosmic order.

For atheists and agnostics, he is largely nothing. For the modern secular person, he is an interesting person who makes rather outrageous claims about himself that they find hard to give credit to. For the modern man and woman, the world is comprised of the natural order, and the Biblical worldview, as represented by Jesus Christ, is quaint, interesting, and largely outdated.

Yet, Jesus of Nazareth retains a great attraction, if not compulsion, for many people to this day, both in the West and in the Third World, Asia and Africa.

The question is Who is He?

Let's take a walk through the Gospel of Matthew as an example and see what it says about Jesus Christ and what he did. In the second chapter of Matthew, Matthew says that three wise men came to Jesus at his birth, guided by a star. In the first chapter of Matthew, Matthew states that Jesus was born of a Virgin and was conceived by the Holy Spirit. Jesus' life there begins with two miraculous events, birth without the aid of a human father and a star in the sky guiding sages to his birthplace in Bethlehem. In the third chapter of Matthew, Jesus is baptized and at that time the spirit of God descends on him and says He is pleased with Jesus. In the fourth chapter of Matthew, Jesus is represented as tempted by Satan and offered the kingdoms of the world if he will fall down and worship Satan. Jesus declines the invitation. In the fifth chapter of Matthew, Jesus engages in some rather cryptic statements saying that the poor in spirit are blessed; the meek will inherit the earth; and those who mourn shall be comforted. In that same chapter, Jesus says that being angry with your brother is the same as killing him and looking at a woman with lust is the commission of adultery in your heart. He also says that everyone who divorces his wife, except on the ground of unchastity, makes her an adulteress.

Jesus says in the seventh chapter of Matthew that the gate is narrow and the way is hard that leads to life and those that find it are few. In the eighth chapter of Matthew, Jesus cleanses a leper. In that same chapter, he heals a centurion's servant, by saying a word. In the eighth chapter, Matthew reports Jesus as calming the raging sea. In the ninth chapter of Matthew, he cures a paralytic, stating that his sins are forgiven. In chapter ten of the Gospel of Matthew, the Apostle reports Jesus as saying that he comes not to bring peace, but a sword, and that he has come to set a man against his father. In the twelfth chapter, Matthew says a blind and dumb man is made to speak by Jesus and regains his sight. In chapter 16 of the Gospel of Matthew, Jesus is reported as feeding five thousand people with five loaves of bread and two fishes, one of many miracles attributed to Jesus of Nazareth. Also, in this chapter, Jesus is reported by the Apostle Matthew as saying, whoever will save his life will lose it, and whoever will lose his life for his sake will find it. In the seventeenth chapter of Matthew, Jesus is transfigured on a mountain, shines like the sun, and his garments become white as light, and Moses and Elijah appear talking with him. In the eighteenth chapter of Matthew, Jesus tells people to become like children to enter the kingdom of Heaven.

In the twenty-first chapter of Matthew, Jesus drives the money changers from the temple and heals the blind and the lame. Finally, at the end, Jesus is crucified, as a criminal, and in Matthew, appears again to his disciples, resurrected from the grave.

What are we to make of this person who says that he has control over nature and over death itself? For many he is a myth. After all, people reason, how can one person defy the laws of nature and claim to be God himself and overcome death. These stories are clearly myths, some say. Myths, I think, are different. The anthropomorphic myths of the Greeks, in which their gods engage in comic and antic peccadilloes, bear no resemblance to the elevated ethical teachings and claims of Jesus of Nazareth.

The basic and fundamental point is, either Jesus said what he said and did what he did, or he didn't. The adventures of Zeus and the Roman Jupiter and Apollo bear little or no resemblance to the profound sayings and events found in the Gospels. I have looked at a few of the sayings, deeds, and events in Jesus' life, as reported in the Gospel of Matthew. Jesus of Nazareth is either insane or crazy, or what he said and did was true. Despite the technologically advanced age in which we live, the person of Jesus Christ and Jesus of Nazareth continues to attract people. He offers them, integrity, love, and valuation that no other system of thought or person offers. He makes an outrageous and insane claim to be God himself and the way to God. Whether we accept or reject that claim, it must be said that no man or woman is intellectually in court unless they examine that claim and determine why, after 2000 years, this man brings people to his person and personhood, as no other person in history has ever done.

Karl Marx in the 19th Century wrote the *Communist Manifesto*. He thought he had a solution for the world's ills. Communism is now gone and passé, and has had its day. Adam Smith wrote T*he Wealth of Nations* defining Capitalism, and one must wonder whether that system will outlast 2000 years of dynamic, growing, and compelling Christianity, which finds its basis, not in a book, not in a car, nor in any thing, but in a person. It is that person with whom we, all of us, must at some point in our lives come to terms.

4. *The Idea of a Christian Society*

In our modern, secular, society, based on material wealth ands goods acquisition, the Christian dogma and faith has, to some extent, lost its societal connection. In short, for many, if not most, Christianity, at best, is little understood or not understood at all. It may be said that the Christian worldview has lost its meaning and attraction for many and is in societal disconnection and disfunctionality. For England's greatest poet, after Shakespeare, John Milton, the author of the only epic poem in English, *Paradise Lost*, the rebellion of Lucifer, the fall of man into sin, and mankind's redemption through the Christ-cross event where the essential and seminal historical events. This, there is, at the present time, some confusion as to what may be said to constitute the idea and ideal of a Christian society.

This is so, not only by reason of the forces of secularism and media and political propaganda, but also the position of certain conservative Protestant denominations, as well as some Roman Catholics, that certain aspects of sexual morality constitute the sole Christian ethical worldview. This is a mistake. It is true, I think, that a Christian society, should it ever come to pass, would include some sort of family structure.

Second, more importantly, the Christian worldview includes a great and pressing concern for the poor, disadvantaged, and the underclass, as reflected in the parable of the Good Samaritan (Luke 10:25) and the story of the rich young man whom Jesus told that in order to follow Him, he must sell all his materials goods. This particular encounter in the Gospels perhaps is best and better understood as meaning that if we are to follow Christ we must give up whatever may impede us in that respect, whether material goods or intellectual pride. Jesus pronounced, in the Beatitudes, the poor and/or poor in spirit as blessed.

Having said this, I think the second prong of a fully developed Christian society would include some sort of utopian or socialistic communal living, giving, and sharing, as is reflected in the earliest Christian communities, as described in the Book of Acts. Unfortunately, at least in the United States, Christianity has long been associated with the capitalist system. This is an error, since Christianity most certainly has no connection with any political or economic system. In the past, Christianity was connected with a monarchy, or the state. There are still state-connected churches in Europe, whether in the United Kingdom or Scandinavia. It has been proven that established churches result in less apprehension of the Christian message. As I said, Christianity has no particular connection with any political or economic system, whether socialism, capitalism, monarchy, or even democracy.

I do think that the idea of a Christian society would tend to some form of commonality and shared giving, rather than the competitive and greed-based basis informing and underlying capitalism. What then must be said of the idea and ideal of a possible Christian society should it ever come to pass? I tend to think it would include both the traditional family structure and some sort of, for want of a better word, socialism, based on community sharing and giving.

5. *The Measure of God's Love*

To understand the nature of God's love in Christ is, at best, difficult since human love, at best or at least our experience of it in this life, is limited and ephemeral. The truth and the fact of the matter is, that with the exception of a few outstanding and exceptional individuals such as Mother Teresa and Albert Schweitzer, most of us may, to some extent, manage to love our children, perhaps our parents, and possibly our spouse, although the latter has proved to be problematical given the number of marriages that fail and result in divorce. For most men and women, that is love's end and maximum extension in this life. Some do not even attain to that level of love. Fathers fail to support their children and mothers abandon their children. Children may consign their elderly parents to a home, rather than undertaking any care giving responsibility.

What then are we to say of God's love in Christ? It is commonplace to say that it is unconditional and eternal.

Perhaps we can best understand and embrace God's love in Christ in that He Himself, in Christ, in His love, took upon and suffered the pangs, torture, and sufferings of dying and death, dying not for one particular person, whom he may have liked well enough, but for all men and women, past, present, and future generations.

We can only understand the depth and extension of God's love in Christ if we ask ourselves honestly whom we would voluntarily die and suffer for, whether our mother, father, children, or spouse, let alone choose to die for persons hardly known to us, and for those whom we may be affirmatively indifferent to, or not like.

The truth of it is, most men and women are intensely selfish and self involved, largely declining to include within their personal orbit most others than their immediate family, let alone choosing to die for them.

What is the measure of God's love in Christ, as opposed to human love? Its measure is that it does not stop at taking on death itself. God's love in Christ does not come to us and is not given to us because we are so lovable and deserving of it. We are not. We are egomaniacs, who will grow old, become unattractive, and ultimately die. We hardly deserve the undying and eternal love of God in Christ. God loves us, in Christ, because His nature is love. He loved us first, and continues to love us, not because of who we are, but because of who He is, the source of life and love itself.

6. Is Poverty Blessed?

During his earthly life, Jesus of Nazareth is recorded as having said many things to many different audiences. Many of these sayings can best be termed cryptic and radical. In the Gospel of Matthew, for example, Jesus is reported to have said:

Do not think that I have come to bring peace on earth; I have not come to bring peace, but a sword. For I have come to set a man against his father, and a daughter against her mother, and a daughter-in-law against her mother-in-law; and a man's foes will be those of his own household. He who loves father or mother more than me is not worthy of me; and he who loves son or daughter more than me is not worthy of me; and he who does not take his cross and follow me is not worthy of me. He who finds his life will lose it, and he who loses his life for my sake will find it. (Matthew 10:34-39)

Obviously, the saying of the Apostle of love that he wishes to not bring peace, but a sword, and to set fathers and daughters against each other is extremely puzzling. It is beyond the scope of this particular essay to try to explain this particular passage. This literary excursus will attempt to explain and focus on Jesus' sayings in the Beatitudes, which Matthew 5:3 reports Jesus as saying "Blessed are the poor in spirit, for theirs is the Kingdom of Heaven," and Luke reports Christ as saying simply "Blessed are the poor," (Luke 6:20). The term "poor in spirit" may be interpreted as meaning humble as opposed to arrogant or prideful. However one may cut it, these are extremely puzzling statements.

For the idea that poverty or humility are somehow blessed estates runs strictly counter to our present society's current emphasis on the good and desirability of the acquisition of material wealth, which permits those who succeed in this enterprise to obtain a measure of dominance, if not arrogance. Clearly, the acquisition of large amounts of wealth, can be hardly thought to result in humility.

Therefore, we must ask in what sense does Jesus mean that poverty and humility are blessed?

I think and believe that great material wealth presents a barrier to faith, belief, and spirituality. For those who acquire great wealth may erroneously come to believe they are all powerful, autonomous, and independent beings, and can come to reject the notion of an invisible God, who has created, rules, and will come to judge, his dependent, created, creatures.

Great material wealth allows us to come to believe in ourselves alone. With wealth and goods, we no longer may feel the need for repentance, salvation, worship, or service, and we surely do not come to feel and exercise great humility.

Wealth, in some sense, is a barrier to personal growth, since it fools us into believing, not in God, but in ourselves as gods, in ourselves alone. Wealth may fool us into believing in a kind of temporary earthly mortality, when the truth of it is that in any second of our lives, we may be taken and removed from the little drama and play that constitutes our lives, bringing us to an abrupt end.

Poverty and humility, Jesus means, is blessed because it enables us to face our limited humanity and basic powerlessness, and the reality that we are forever set on the precipice of tomorrow.

This saying of Christ is radical, puzzling, and shocking, since in thought he sets himself and the Church against the values of the secular and material society in materialism, power, pride, and arrogance. How then is poverty and humility blessed and why are those states blessed?

They are blessed because the truth is that we do not run the show and we all share, at best, a limited life span, or in a word and better put, a short spree of immortality. Wealth leads us to believe in our personal power and immortality, when the truth is that each day we live on borrowed time.

7. A Few False Idols

We, all of us, as we go through our lives, often seek to uplift ourselves above the crowd, or, better put, seek to nail and found our self-confidence or personhood on some personal quality, accomplishment, or whatever we might want to pin our hopes on.

Many, if not most, pin their sense of self-importance, particularly in the present age, on their material wealth or riches. They say to others, my superiority or greatness lies in my expensive car, perhaps a Lexus, BMW, or Mercedes, or my expensive vacation home in the Hamptons.

Others prefer to point to themselves on other bases. One group seeks to uplift themselves by saying, "I am smarter than other people or better educated." They may point out to others that they have specialized knowledge in some certain field, and so they convince themselves they are in some way so much superior to the "lesser minds" that surround them.

A third group of folks adopt another way of raising themselves above the crowd. They will point to the fact that they are cultured and better educated, and by this method, they see others, and label them at least in their own minds, as ignorant or unlettered.

The fourth group, may say to the world, "I have greater physical strength." Football players and athletes may seek to dominate their environment by this method.

For a fifth group, it may be their appearance or looks that enable them to say to themselves, "I am better than other people." This is particularly prevalent in our present society. It makes victims, by this false standard, of both women and men.

The sixth group, and this is a particularly sad commentary, may claim that they are morally superior; perhaps they may say, "I have great religious faith," and for these folks their greater virtue, morality, or faith, at least as they believe, separate them from the crowd.

These modes of pinning our hopes on some quality or accident attached to ourselves is, I think, fallacious. For the true believing Christian, God attaches value to all souls and all people, regardless of their economic status, culture, appearance, physical strength, intelligence, education, or, if you will, their faith.

In short, one might say, that God attaches greater value to one soul that comes to him, than all the culture, wealth, intellect, knowledge, beauty, or strength that others may have.

Let me end this little essay by saying that when I was a younger person I thought culture, education, and perhaps religious faith might be important, or at least I sought to make myself important by these methods. I now know this was a mistake. In fact, by making culture, education, or religious faith a kind of idol, I mistook their use and purpose. Culture, as a term, has no particular meaning beyond the fact that some people, if not many people, enjoy particular artistic products. The goal is the natural enjoyment of those works, rather than the use of them to separate and exclude others. By the same token, religious faith, or Christian belief, is not to be used as a method of barring and excluding the unsaved, but is rather a good thing in that it makes us better people and makes for a better life for us and the people around us.

It is a grievous and sad commentary that humanity uses the many goods that surround them as a method of dominance, exclusion, and the establishment of class demarcations. That is neither the use nor the purpose of the particular qualities and goods that I have just discussed. As usual, any good is corrupted by twisted human nature.

8. Some Few Words about Love, or A Meditation on Love

In the modern world, love is a word much bandied about and loosely used. We are bombarded in the media, and a popular culture, with songs, visions, and pictures of what is presented as love.

People seek for love in the unlikeliest of places, whether bars or bookstores. Some, in a desperate search for what is, after all, simple human companionship, resort to personal advertisements, a product of the alienation, disconnection, and loneliness characteristic of capitalist, western culture, most particularly in the huge impersonal urban areas.

When we speak of love, most have reference to romantic love, closely associated with marriage. The idea of romantic love has its origins in the Middle Ages tradition of courtly love, and this romantic ideal of marriage, and the relations between the sexes, served to fuel both the literature and relationships of western culture for some fifteen hundred years.

This ideal, however, has been decimated, if not destroyed, by the feminist movement, the notion of total blending, sameness, and equality of the sexes; the sexual revolution,; and the frank animalism that has come to dominate all forms of imaginative literature, both print and visual. If we have not grown up from the ideal of romantic love, at least we have grown away from it. Who shall be the gainer or loser in this process, who can say?

Of course it must be said that for our ancestors and for much of the world, outside the West, marriage has been and continues to be largely an economic exchange, a matter of a pure business transaction between families, having nothing to do at all with the romantic ideal of sex and marriage that was prevalent in Western culture, at least until 1960.

Romantic love, or better put sexual erotic love, can be confused and incorrectly apprehended by those in its throes, associated as it is with possessiveness, jealousy, control, and dominance. Moreover, confused by the temporary excitement of erotic love we may be led to what is not, truly, love at all.

Erotic love, however, is one of many loves that we may come to know and apprehend throughout our lifetimes.

There is the love between friends, a meeting and sharing of like minds and personal perspectives. This is the least controlling of loves and has an equality, a mutuality of sharing that is lacking in erotic romantic love, focused as it is on possessing and having the lover beyond all.

The strongest and most sacrificial of loves is the love of a parent for a child. This is unconditional and seeks no recompense or return. It is all giving with no expectation of gaining a return.

And then there is a love between siblings, sister and brother, brother and brother, sister and sister, founded and based on affection. There is even love for the subhuman, our pet, dog or cat, who may be our most faithful companion, giving us its unconditional companionship, loyalty, and love.

There is also the love of nature, which can be and is often expressed in great poetry. Sad to say, this love is increasingly unavailable to the modern urban dweller, who is afforded little chance or opportunity to see the stars, a sunset, or the green flowered fields.

Finally, we come to charity, the love of God. This is the greatest of loves, seeking the good of others for no reason. God is love and, in loving us, seeks and brings us to share his love as his creatures. In the midst of this literary excursus on love and the forms of love, one must observe that for most of us we confuse love with receiving, apprehending, and obtaining it from others.

For many of us, this is what we think love is, being in love. This is the selfish love of the child who assumes that he is entitled to undivided love and attention. This is a fallacy and misconception. Love is giving and seeking the good of another, enriching and uplifting without tainted egotism or without any notion of self-enrichment. In this sense, the love of a parent for a child and the love of God for his creatures and creation is the most real of loves, involving as it does giving, caring, and sacrificing with no expectation or idea of return or recompense.

At the end of it all, the loves we have and have built through our lifetime are crushed and taken from us by death. Death may take our beloved child in its infancy; we know our parents will die; our spouse may die before us, that person whom we thought to marry may be taken from us in the midst of life. Death ends not only our lives, but the structures of all loves that we have labored to build.

For the Christian, there is an ultimate answer to the destruction in death of our loves and beloved. God is love. He creates us and sustains us, not because he needs us, but because he wants to share his endless, infinite, and abounding mercy and love. In Christ we are shown the face of God's cosmic love.

The Psalms are said to be the oldest of Biblical texts, dating to 500 B.C. and some few are reputed to have been actually authored by King David of Israel. In Psalm 89:48 the Psalmist asks the question that seems to end and crush all our loves, "What man is he that liveth, and shall not see death."

The answer of Christ that assures us that our lives and loves will not come to nothing and that in the end, love is the conqueror, is a statement, "I am the man in whom whosoever abideth, shall not see death." One might safely say that since God is love that the only place outside of heaven where we can be safe from the dangers and pangs of love is in hell itself.

9. *Hell and Damnation*

The Doctrine of Hell, Damnation, Perdition, or eternal punishment is an integral Doctrine of the Christian faith. It has the support of Holy Scripture, the words and admonitions concerning it, to that effect, by our Lord, and is fully articulated in the Creedal Affirmations of the Church.

The idea behind the Doctrine is that at the end of time there will be a last judgment by the returned Christ, and that all men and women will, in some sense, be judged on the basis of their lives, works, and apprehension of the Christian faith during their lives. Some will enter into the joys of paradise and eternal loving communion with God and Christ. The others will be condemned to eternal death and punishment. The idea and Doctrine of eternal punishment is, in many ways, an outrage and an unacceptable concept. That a loving and merciful God should condemn the creatures, whom he created out of love and sent his only begotten son to live for and then to die a tortured death by the Roman death penalty of crucifixion, is beyond belief or human understanding.

If I could eliminate this Doctrine from the Christian dogmatic system, I would gladly do so with all my heart.

Origen, a leading Christian thinker of the 4th Century A.D., posited universal salvation. He was condemned as a heretic. I offer here, three justifications for this most devastating and unacceptable of dogmas.

First, all of us, as persons, are given some and a certain time to live in this life. For some it is short; others longer; and others even longer. We do not know the reason for this.

We do know this much. For the time we are given in this life, however long or short, we have the opportunity to shape, create, and form ourselves. If, in this life, we be arrogant, cruel, selfish, egotistical, unkind, unforgiving, taking and not giving, avaricious, greedy, gossipy, sharp tongued, satirical, and backbiting, so we will be forever, and so we will be with others who are the same as us.

If we be charitable, loving, giving, forgiving, tolerant, humble, desiring to serve, tender of others' feelings, disinclined to hurt, kind, and generous, so we will be ourselves forever, and so will we be with others like us.

In the timeline we are given, however short or long, we can in some sense become unmade and inauthentic men and women or rise to the greatness of soul and spirit prepared and made possible for us.

We can shrink to negative being and nothingness in this life, having devoted our lives solely to ourselves and no others, or we can be what we are meant to be. What we have grown to be in this short lifespan, so will we be forever.

Thus, no one is sent to hell or condemned to it by a merciful and loving God, but in some sense, walk there by the choices they make in this life.

Thus, Hell is not so much a condemnation or judgment on our failed humanity, but the end result of what in this life we have chosen to be.

Second, the image of Hell as a place of torment and torture is an image only.

If anything, Hell is isolation, loneliness, and separation from love. In the absence of love, in a real sense, we have no existence, or better put, an inauthentic, twisted, or degraded existence. Hell is being cut off. It is spending the rest of our lives for eternity with people like ourselves: greedy, selfish, arrogant, egotistical, callous, and indifferent. It is being condemned for eternity to be surrounded with others like ourselves and to be condemned to be only with ourselves and no others.

We will be condemned to exist for eternity in Hell, so the doctrine states. We will not die because a loving God does not destroy his creatures. He allows and permits them to live their lives, cut off from joy and the communion of life.

Third, God is a God of justice, as well as mercy and love. Mankind fell from paradise into sin. The death and resurrection of Jesus Christ occurred to end this separation. God gives us free will and choice. He does not want his creation and creatures to be automatons or robots. He gives us the option and choice of choosing Him over mammon, greed, selfishness, egotism, and materialism. What we choose, so we will be.

Fourth, there are many Protestant Fundamentalists who delight in condemning the large portion of humanity, the so-called unsaved others, to Hell. Hell is not about Hitler or Stalin. It is not about our nasty neighbor, or our unremitting boss.

This warning of Our Lord is not about those other unkind and mean people we talk about and criticize and condemn and attack. It is about ourselves.

10. Who Reads the Bible and Why

The Bible is a very old document; in fact, it is an ancient book. Some of it dates back to 1500 B.C. in its present written form.

It consists of the Hebrew Scriptures, or Old Testament, which claims to be God's covenant and dealings with the people of Israel. The New Testament is the narrative of the life of Jesus of Nazareth, his death and resurrection, message, deeds, and sayings, as well a number of letters and documents tracing the growth and history of the early church, in the Book of Acts, and the development of Christian Doctrine, particularly in the Pauline Epistles.

For a long time, particularly for English-speaking Protestants, and more particularly in America, the Bible was the most important and widely read of books, well into the conclusion of the 19th Century, particularly in the form of the Authorized, or King James', Version of the Bible of 1611.

Sad to say, this is no longer the case. The Bible, at the present time, is read, at least in the Western world of Europe, the United States, Canada, Australia, and New Zealand, by a minority.

Certainly it is rarely read, if at all, by the intellectual elite or persons with some degree of education.

This is not surprising in light of the scientific, medical, technological, and economic progress and growth that offer people a level of comfort and prosperity in this life that mutes the offer of eternal life through Christ which the Bible offers.

Who then reads the Bible and why?

There is one group, and this is by far the largest in this modern age and society, that either do not know of the Bible or have no interest in reading it. They may be said to be indifferent to the Bible.

In fact, this group are indifferent to most old books and literature, whether Homer, Shakespeare, Spenser, the Greek Tragedy of Aeschylus, Euripides, and Sophocles, or even Jane Austen and Charles Dickens.

Their lives are blissful and happy, albeit uninformed. Their ideas, principles, and guiding thoughts, if they exist, result and come from some sort of osmosis or process of absorption from what the media, computers, and television may offer them.

If they are offered sexual freedom or promiscuity, they take hold of it. If they are offered the materialism and greed of President Bush, Vice President Cheney, and corporate America, they apprehend this as a model, giving no thought or concern that greed and avarice are hardly guiding life principles or role models.

The idea that there is anything in them that is wrong and that requires repair, intervention, or fixing by an eternal God or, in fact, that their lives are empty and that they are failed beings and not autonomous, but dependent, creatures, never occurs to them. They are content to spend their lives getting as much sex and money as they can get, little knowing or caring that eternity awaits them.

How can, to these persons, a book of apparent silly myths have any relevance to their latest purchase of a Lexus, their meal in an expensive restaurant, or their outing with a beautiful woman with whom they are about to entertain themselves. This is the first group.

The second group are those who read the Bible as a work of literature, particularly in the form of the Authorized Version of 1611. They are a very thin minority. It is true that the Bible contains much great prose and poetry. Indeed, I would challenge anyone to tell me which they would soon grow tired of, the Psalms, in their English translation, or Plato, in an English translation.

Most people, who read the Bible as literature, might read it in a college or graduate level course. In fact, there are very few people who read and apprehend the Bible as literature.

I think this is so, because the Bible, as a book, was not meant to be literature, but a revelation of God's intervention and acts in human history and more ultimately a guide and advisement of how we should live our lives ethically and morally and, most importantly, of how we may obtain eternal life through faith in the crucified and risen Jesus Christ.

In short, I think, the Bible is little read as literature because it is not meant to be literature.

Now we come to the third group. This is by far the largest group of Bible readers. These persons read the Bible as the revelation by God as to how they should live and what they should believe to be true about lasting, ultimate, and important things. These people read the Bible to find out what life means, how and what they should believe, and what they may be able to attain in the end as human beings.

The Bible must always be read by persons, whoever, wherever, and whatever they are—whether in Africa, China, India, or the United States, or England or Germany—as the revelation by God concerning his covenant with the Jewish people and his new covenant of Jesus Christ, concerning what we should do in this life, what we should believe about God, and how we may come to eternal life and glory in the company of righteous, loving, persons, in continued love and relationship with the triune God, and those who have chosen to be with him in paradise.

The only reason to read the Bible, this group rightly concludes, is because it is true and will always and forever supersede any temporary source of truth or, better put, whatever happens to be faddish or fashionable.

The works, acts, and sayings of Jesus Christ offer us eternal life. His ethics are a higher ethic that have ever been stated and that none of us are or will be able to attain.

He counsels us to moral perfection, to love our neighbors as ourselves, to give away our riches and material goods and embrace poverty; he tells us that to look at a woman with lust is to commit adultery, and that if our eye offends us, to pluck it out; we are told not to judge others.

No Greek thinker, Plato or Aristotle, said or offered anything close to this in their system of thought.

The Bible will always be read by those who wish to know and understand ultimate truth about who we are, what we should do with our lives, and where we are going.

This minority of Bible readers, however large or small, will read the Bible for what is meant to be, not as literature and not as an old and irrelevant old book, hardly competition for the Internet or cable television, but for what it is, the sum of the revelation from the eternal God to a failed, broken, twisted, and misdirected humanity in need of restoration and regeneration—in a word salvation.

11. Whatever Happened to Sin and Evil

It started with Freud and Jung, this abdication of personal responsibility. We began to blame our rage, wrongdoing, and hostility on what our mothers, fathers, and lovers did or did not do for us or with us. Our primal urges, perhaps misdirected, misplaced, or spurned and rejected, served to excuse and explain our wayward, and even abnormal conduct. The Blacks and Latinos blame Caucasian gentry for their second class underclass status and poverty breeding crime. Women blame men for their second class historical status and let it serve to excuse any lack of civility or courtesy and, on the part of some few, outright hostility. Homosexuals say it is a gene that separates them from the heterosexual majority.

In a word, it would appear, that any disaffected person or group may, if not excuse, then explain away any anger, rage, or even wrongdoing through the accidents of history or biological chance.

Perhaps it is true that we all bear the burden of our past and our biology and cannot escape our destinies. Perhaps it is true that we all are predestined by historical forces, or the sum total of our past experience, to be unkind, unforgiving, merciless, uncompassionate, and even evildoers.

The question is what is left of our freedom, or better put, our capacity for free choice and free will to make voluntary ethical choices.

Opposed to the choices of hostility and wrongdoing are compassion and charity, I think. I am safe to say that I would regard it as old fashioned in this respect, but the choices of good and evil constitute the freedom to be fully human or less so. Hostility, hate, and evil, for Saint Augustine, had no existence. The world, unfortunately, consists not only of Hitlers and Stalins, but of Albert Schwietzers and Mother Teresas.

Are we simply predestined by external and internal forces to be what we are or are we made, whatever we are, by choices of good and evil? In short, are we victims or free beings?

I argue that we must recognize in our worldview the existence of good, evil, and in a word, sin and Satan, as opposed to goodness and truth. To abandon the existence and reality of sin and evil, and blame these impulses on genetic or environmental factors, is to degrade our humanity, the humanity that erected the cathedrals of Europe and wrote the *Divine Comedy*.

We all have our choices of sin and death in this life or goodness and light. Once we are relieved of the right and responsibility to make free choices, we are no more than things in the clutches of life. Free ethical choice recognizes the darkness that lies within our souls. Sad to say, Saint Francis of Assisi and John Milton do and have occupied the same planetary space with Lenin and Pol Pot. We fail as men and women when we explain away Darfur and the Armenian Genocide through a deprived childhood and misdirected sexuality.

The time now is that we must recognize the reality of sin and evil, underplayed since Marx and Freud. It is right and appropriate that once and for all we recognize not only the right and responsibility to make moral choices, but our capacity to do so. No one can be forced to choose and no more can we explain our wrong choices by blaming others. Sin and evil are within our grasp as well as kindness and compassion. To me it is significant that although our modern presidents write self-praising autobiographies in a shallow and vain attempt to present and preserve what they perceive as their greatness, John Bunyan, the great writer and author of *The Pilgrim's Progress* entitled his spiritual autobiography *Grace Abounding to the Chief of Sinners.* Whatever happened to sin and evil? They are alive and well in Iraq.

12. Prayer and Petition

As Christians, we are told by Jesus of Nazareth to pray. He even gave us a prayer, which we call the Lord's Prayer, as a guide to what we should say.

Since its inception, some 2000 years ago, to this day, Christianity has been a praying faith. Christians have been instructed to pray not only in their churches, but in their homes. We are told to pray as a conduit to God and Christ, and to do it constantly and regularly.

Yet, it occurs to me as somewhat strange, if not paradoxical, that an omnipotent and omniscient God, who exists in eternity, who has heard all prayers of all men and women from the beginning of time to its end, in one tableaux, who knows the prayer before it is spoken and knows the answer He has given, if any, still commands us to pray.

Moreover, this all powerful and omnipotent being wishes not only to be petitioned, but praised. Is God and Christ some sort of Santa Claus who divvies out gifts to his select favorites who ask him with sufficient and persistent effort? Is God and Christ some sort of egomaniac and so insecure that He requires to be praised? The answer to these questions lies in our relationship to God and Christ, or better put, in the nature of our relationship. God, as he is apprehended in Jesus Christ, wishes us to communicate with Him. In a word, He wants relationships with his creatures or, more simply put, wants friends. He wants to share, with no gain in sight for Himself, His undying and infinite love with us as His sons and daughters.

By praying we approach God and Christ, and He embraces us. Prayer is a form of sharing. It is relating to our creator in need and love, and in turn being enfolded by that love.

In prayer, we rise above our limited selves in time and become in some sense little Christs or the persons who we are capable of being.

When we pray, we attach ourselves to the risen Christ and in some sense are able to share His being and love and to be remade and reborn in His image.

Prayer is a catalyst that enables us to grow to be in the image of Christ.

We do not always know the answer the we are given to our petition or, better put from our perspective, the answer we want; we do not always know what is the purpose of praying and petitioning. We know this much however, from our earthly lives, that without communication there is no relationship or relationships. God wants relationships. He wants us as friends and wants to share with us His love and being. He sent His only begotten son to a twisted and degraded humanity in order to have relationships with us and to share.

When we pray, we grow in our relationship with Christ, or better put, when we communicate we have that relationship. Christ wants to share His love, not on the basis of force, but by having us reach out to Him as a product of our free will, not obtained by force or compulsion, since relationships by force are no relationships at all. No woman can love the man who raped her, or the child love the parent who abuses him or her. Prayer is the catalyst and mode of friendship and relationship with God and Christ.

13. Suffering and Pain: A Tentative Answer

We, all of us, as human beings know that in this life we will, to some degree and extent, suffer and endure pain, whether physical or emotional. The pain and suffering we will come to endure throughout our lives at various times from birth to death is an ever present reality. We come to this life in pain, and in the process of living, and then dying, we are inflicted with pain and suffering.

Some pain we cannot escape. This pain and suffering comes upon us through agencies beyond our control, such as disease, illness, or natural disasters, i.e. earthquakes, volcanoes, tornados, hurricanes, or pestilence. On the other hand, most of the pain and suffering that come upon us as human beings, comes to us through human actions and agencies—wars, crime, the cruelty of our spouse who knows us well enough to know every weakness, or at our jobs, through the power wielded by those above us. The fact of the matter is that our fellow human beings, given power over us, will often cause us pain and suffering. It is only men that who invented the whip, the rack, the hangman's noose and the electric chair.

In this essay, I will examine why I think we suffer as human beings and the cause and reason for pain and suffering in this life.

First, let me begin by saying that I, who have endured little or no physical or emotional pain and have hardly suffered in my life, am hardly in a position to comment or speak on or to this issue. I have never known the pain of the terminally ill cancer patient. One can say, I admit, that my thoughts on this subject have a hollow ring.

Nevertheless, I will try to give some thoughts on why we as human beings must suffer and the use and reason for pain and suffering.

Let me attempt to explain involuntary pain, or the pain that comes upon us in natural events. For the Christian, this pain is thought to result from our fallen humanity, or, better put, our degraded and corrupt human nature. One might say that in the fall of Adam into death and sin, our otherwise perfect relationship with God the Creator was twisted and shattered, with the result that pain and suffering came into the world that formerly knew nothing of pain, whether pain in the form of a natural disaster, the pain of childbirth, or the pain associated with death and dying. This, one can say, is the involuntary infliction of pain and can be said to result from our broken relationship with our Creator.

This is one, albeit perhaps unacceptable and weak, explanation of the presence of involuntary pain and suffering in the world, however tentative, inadequate, or inexplicable.

Having, to some extent, explained the involuntary presence of pain and suffering in the world, I would say the explanation is lame, since a merciful and compassionate God, whose love is so great that it did not stop at the sacrifice, torture, and death at the cross of the Son of God for all humankind who neither knew him, were indifferent to him, rejected him, nor loved him in return or at all, allows this pain to permeate our earthly lives and actually end them. I offer here a number of explanations.

First, I think I am safe in saying that if we do not suffer and experience some pain in the course of our earthly lives, we do not grow and develop as human beings. Suffering allows us to develop compassion for those around us, for their tribulations, and for their sufferings that otherwise, there is some chance, we would not be able to apprehend. I think it is a sure thing that we do not grow and love, or are not able to love, absent pain and suffering in our earthly lives. Without suffering and pain we remain selfish and egocentric, never fully understanding the suffering and pain of our fellow beings. In this sense, pain is a tool enabling us to grow as persons in love, understanding, and compassion.

Second, Christ, the paragon and model of the new man or woman, or the image of the new creation, took pain and suffering upon himself. From eternity, he chose to lower himself to take on human form and limitation. He had no wealth or power in his earthly life and chose to be a carpenter, or more exactly put, a working man. He died a most ghastly and awful death of slow and agonizing crucifixion. He did all this out of love for all past, present, and future of generations and human beings who did not know him at all, perhaps did not and do not love him, and have rejected and continue to reject him.

We cannot apprehend Christ, or his underlying mercy and love, without also taking upon ourselves in some fashion this pain, sacrifice, and suffering. We cannot grasp and understand his eternal sacrifice and love without doing the same.

Third, although this life has its share of natural pain which we cannot control or avoid, nevertheless it must be said that much pain comes from the malice and wickedness of others who inflict pain on those around them on a regular, constant, and it is safe to say, historical basis. We cannot blame God for allowing pain when he grants us freedom of choice and free will. We may choose in our relationships with others to ignore their needs and choose not to relieve their pain, or even deliberately cause others pain by our acquisition of power and position over them.

The history of the world is filled with torture, slavery, oppression, war, and genocides, and continues to be so. We cannot blame God for our free choice of wickedness and evil.

Pain originally came into our fallen world and continues to be caused by ourselves on a continuous basis. Withal, the Creator, as he does with all things and events, uses pain for his own purposes, so that we come to know, by and through pain, the bases and wellspring of love, compassion, charity, and mercy that if we are totally protected and barricaded in our lives, we would never come to know.

Pain comes from our corrupt, twisted, and degraded human nature and, in a turnaround, makes us fully human, enabling us to overcome our selfishness and self-love. In pain we take up the cross that leads us to eternal life and eternal love, a life without suffering and pain. One is safe in saying that one can only reach love and relationship through sacrifice and, to some extent, suffering and sorrow.

It is significant that the love of the mother, the highest and most elevated forms of our earthly loves, can only be attained through the pain and suffering of pregnancy and childbirth and a life of nurturing, sacrifice, and unconditional love and giving.

It is only in pain, that we can come to know ourselves truly and deeply, come to know others, and come to know Jesus Christ, the image of eternal and undying love.

14. Priests or Priestesses

At this particular point in history, the Roman Catholic Church, the Greek Orthodox Church, and certain Protestant sects such as the Southern Baptists and Missouri-Synod Lutherans do not ordain women as priests or ministers.

The feminist movement is vociferous, zealous, and unremitting in its condemnation of what they perceive as unfair and outdated dogma, having its origins in an older and ancient patriarchal society.

At first glance the feminists, or rather women who are critical of this exclusionary rule, may be right. After all, why bar a committed Christian who wishes to serve in and execute this particular office? Why deprive the Church of the talents, contributions, and commitment of half the human race? This argument, or rather criticism of this particular rule of dogma, I submit, fails on a number of grounds.

There are a number of reasons for this particular dogma and those reasons require an understanding of the nature of the priestly or ministerial office and its historical origins and background.

First, the priest or minister who celebrates mass, the Eucharist, or what it is called in the Protestant Church, Communion, stands, in some sense, in the stead and person of Christ. It is not that a woman cannot be a priest or minister, but that she cannot stand in the person of the Divine Savior who revealed himself in his earthly life as a male, and, as risen, sits at the right hand of God, the Father, in some sort of contiguous spiritual male body. Thus, it is safe to say that the nature of the reenactment of the sacrifice of Christ, in some sense, whereby the priest or minister stands in the person of Christ, is a male role. It is not that a woman is disqualified politically, constitutionally, or as a matter of justice or fairness from holding this office, but that the Church, in this particular rule, is not a democracy, nor does it operate under the secular rules of apparent fair play.

Second, the argument that this doctrine has its origins in outdated patriarchy also fails. In fact, a large part of the ancient world and near East including Assyria, Sumerian, and Babylonia, worshipped mother goddesses with outsized genitals and breasts.

Temple prostitution was common and the reason for this worship of the mother goddess had its origin in our forbearers and ancestors not knowing how food was grown. Their simple solution was to connect the seasons and the growth of food with the sexual, biological function. Hence, the very common presence, in most parts of the Ancient world, of mother and female earth goddesses.

Jewish culture, and its outgrowth in Christianity, rejects any connection of God with biology and sex.

If God had chosen to reveal himself in female form, he would connect and lead us to believe that as created beings we are the products of the female maternal and biological function.

In Judaism and Christianity, God chose to reveal himself in male terminology, which is nothing more than an analogy, since God is a spirit, and has no sex or body.

After all, if Jesus was the son of God, and if God chose to reveal himself in female forms and terminology, then God would be a mother and would be bearing children, rather than Jesus being co-equal and connected equally with God and fully God.

In short, for God to be analogized with female sexuality, both we and Jesus would be products of a mother and pregnancy, from whom we came, and to whom, supposedly, we go back to. The ministerial or priestly office is not a job, but a sacerdotal function and vocation, in which the sacrifice of Christ is reenacted and in which God chooses not to mislead us to believe that we share some sort of biological relationship to his being.

We are not born of God, but rather created by an eternal spirit who, by an analogy, chooses to form his relationship through terms of father and son, rather than maternity, pregnancy, and birth.

I would add, however, that a minister in the Protestant Church has a function unlike a priest in the Catholic and Greek Orthodox Church, since strictly speaking he is a leader of a community of Christians, a equal among equals, rather than one who conducts a sacrifice on a weekly or daily basis, as is the case in the Catholic and Greek Orthodox Churches.

15. *The Two Christmases*

In the past 150 years there has been a division in Western society about Christmas. In short, there are two Christmases. One Christmas may be called the secular, or perhaps more exactly put, the commercial Christmas. This Christmas is a time of general good will in which there is a general atmosphere of liking, generosity, and approachability. This Christmas, which has been widely adopted in our culture by all faiths, is closely tied to commerce and money. It is celebrated by merchants who desire to sell as many goods as possible to make money for themselves. It is a rather disturbing commentary that at one time Christmas carols concerning the birth of Christ were played on the radio and television to the general public. Typical carols might have been "Joy to the World," "Little Town of Bethlehem," or "Come All Ye Faithful." These carols have been gradually replaced by more generalized Christmas songs such as "Rudolph the Red nosed Reindeer" or "Santa Claus is Coming to Town."

I think this Christmas of general good will and gift giving, which is closely associated with Christmas trees and Christmas decorations, has its origins in the Pagan world as some sort of winter festival. This Christmas is the Christmas that has come to dominate our Western society, or at least the society in the United States.

There is a second Christmas, however, which is celebrated by a thinner and thinner minority. This minority concerns itself with the birth of Christ, or shall we say, God taking form in a human being. For Christians, Christmas is both a joy and a fear. It is a joy because God entered human history and humanity. It is a fear because it is the recognition that mankind, both man and woman, are misdirected, twisted, corrupt, and in need of help. The true meaning of Christmas has been largely lost in the glitter, noise, and cacophony that assaults all of us in mind, ears, and eyes, from October through January.

Christmas is none of those things. It is God, through part of his being, entering into human history at an exact and discrete point in time. The reason for this entrance is to repair a broken relationship between man and God. It is a time for celebration and joy, as well as a recognition that repair was necessary.

Most, if not all people, reject the Christian Christmas, or are largely indifferent to it. The Christian Christmas is God's making a claim on the human mind and on humanity through his son. We must recognize that most values in the world are erroneous and incorrect. Therefore, the world's rejection of the Christian Christmas, or its indifference to it, is mistaken. The world's values are self-love, dominance, the acquisition of wealth, power, selfishness, and greed. That the world does not recognize the Christian Christmas is an admission on the part of the world system that is completely wrong.

16. The Christian Worldview vs. Secularism, or the Ancient vs. the Modern

Ever since the 18th Century Enlightenment, the Christian worldview has been, if not under attack then, on the wane. With the advent of science, Darwinism, Freud, and the so-called critical method and methodology applied to the Biblical text, the—for want of a better word—Christian worldview has been severely and seriously called into question. Even the formerly magnificent edifice of philosophy has been torn down with the new subjects of science, and now business and computers. Philosophy is virtually left only with metaphysics that is now under serious attack by secularism and materialism. This article proposes to consider and examine what the Christian worldview is, what the worldview of secularism is, and to suggest that the Christian worldview still has validity and truth.

Let us take a look at what may be thought to constitute the Christian worldview in the first instance and see if it still has something to offer us. The Christian worldview starts with creation of the universe by an omniscient and omnipotent God, pure spirit, ex nihilo, reported in Genesis as occurring in seven earthly days. The Creation consists of the creation of the Earth and the Heavens, animal and plant life, and finally, finds it apex in the creation of man, male and female.

The second element of the Christian worldview is the fall of man into sin. In the Christian worldview man was created to exist and commune in a direct and loving relationship with his Father and Creator, God, and fell into sin, tempted by Satan. The fall into sin happened because man sought to be autonomous, independent from God, a ruler in his or her own right. In short and in sum, the fall of man into sin occurred because of his pride.

It follows that the third element of the Christian worldview is the rebellion of Lucifer and his angels, and their being cast into Hell, cut off from God, who is love. The sin of Lucifer was overwhelming and overweening pride that declined to serve or, more aptly put, to be subservient. Satan, or going under his other name Lucifer, would rather, according to Milton, reign in Hell, cut off from life and love, than serve in Heaven.

The fourth element of the Christian worldview is that the fall of mankind into sin brought pain and death in its wake. Human nature was corrupted, the world was twisted and broken, with the result that natural disaster, pain and suffering, and human wickedness and evil came into the picture; these were formerly lacking from the cosmic world order, ordained and created by God. The fall brought about not only death, but a twisted sexuality and the suffering in connection with childbirth.

The fifth element of the Christian worldview is that God made a covenant with the Jewish people to be the conduit and connection of his world and thought and message. In the ancient world, it was only the Jewish people who declined to worship idols and who were not polytheists, but believed in only one God. Their religious ethics declined to include rampant sexual practices, and limited sexual practice to marriage and monogamy. Within the Jewish culture, there were prophets who called Israel to a higher ethic of charity and love for the poor, disadvantaged, and widows.

The sixth element of the Christian worldview is that the Bible is the revealed word of God and contains not a higher ethic commanded upon men and women, but is the revelation of who God is, where the world is going, what men and women should do to live in connection with God and in right connection with themselves.

The seventh element of the Christian worldview is that due to man's fall into sin, God sent his being in the person of Jesus of Nazareth to correct the broken and twisted relationship of man with God. Jesus of Nazareth, according to Christian worldview, was the product of a Virgin birth, did many miracles, mandated a special regard and concern for the poor and a rejection of the accumulation of material wealth as a goal of life, and finally, at the cross and in the crucifixion, was a sacrifice for fallen mankind in their sinful condition, to bring them into correct relationship with God, or more aptly put, to offer them salvation.

The eighth element of the Christian worldview is that Jesus Christ is the only way that we can come to and know God, and that he, after his crucifixion did not die, but rose again from the dead and is presently in Heaven in communion and conversation with the other two persons of the Trinity, the Father and the Holy Spirit.

The Christian worldview maintains that Jesus Christ will come again, this time not in humility, but will come again to judge the world and set up a new world order, a new Heaven, a new Earth. Those who have followed him, and whose lives have been transformed by their relationship with him, will be with him in love and eternal life in Heaven. The others who have rejected him, whether verbally or in their lives, will be cast into Hell where they will never die, but will be cut off from love and community with the men and women who have chosen in their lives to be transformed by His love and to be in a relationship with Him.

This, in a nutshell, is the Christian worldview. I would add that the Christian worldview includes the existence of Satan or Lucifer who wishes to cut off humanity from God and confuse them and bring them to share in his suffering, isolation, loneliness, and hardness of heart.

What are we then to say? To the modern secular man, the Christian worldview appears quaint, old-fashioned, out of connection, and probably slightly ridiculous. The ideas and concepts in the Christian worldview of another world of spirits, of sacrifice, or even of eternal life, are foreign to our society, which says to us that with science and medicine things are getting better and better, and the world is more and more comfortable. For the secular person, life ends in this life and there is nothing more. We are lucky to take what we can get, get as far as we can, do what we can for ourselves, and hope for the best that we will live as long as possible and not die too young as the animals, trees, and plants do. For the modern secular person, there is a life cycle with a beginning, middle, and end.

The person of today, rightly, asks what this world of computers, iPods, DVDs, and globalization has to do with angels, demons, and another world.

The secular worldview would appear to have a degree of validity on the face of it. To the modern man or woman, getting that new house, buying that new car, taking that comfortable vacation, and getting his or her next new DVD or CD is the main thing. It is for the modern man and woman a bit much to believe this "supernatural stuff." I believe the modern secular worldview unfortunately fails in its solution for life's difficulties.

First, it fails to account how we got here or what we are doing here. Personally, I find it hard to believe that I am the product of a long line of ancestors who at first came out of the sea and finally emerged as apes and monkeys. Second, the secular worldview fails to account for sin, wickedness, and evil. Although there has been scientific material and progress in medicine, there has been little spiritual progress. People are regularly massacred in genocides, and frankly, no one much cares. The best that happens is that there is some consideration afterwards given saying, "Well, that's too bad."

The secular worldview fails to take into account or understanding the obvious fact of man's corrupt and defective nature, and frankly, offers little or no solution intellectually or otherwise. It seems to me that men are still the brutes they always have been, out for themselves, out to get for themselves, and out to find ways to squeeze out other people in life's competition for material goods. At best, it may be said that most men and women are merely concerned with going to work and getting their next meal, hardly considering other people outside of themselves. Let me add that I include myself in this analysis and equation and am not sitting in some sort of hypocritical judgment of my fellow men and women.

Third, the secular humanistic worldview fails to deal with mortality and death. Throughout our lives, each of us, man and woman, is on the slow road to death and, for the secular humanistic worldview, extinction. The modern worldview fails to explain death, or deal with it, and shunts it away in hiding to quick funerals in special homes reserved for that purpose. The reality of death in the Western world is well hidden, in contrast to the third world where it is an ever present, constant, and bludgeoning reality. In short, the modern worldview chooses to ignore death and human mortality and offers no explanation beyond nothingness for us all. The Christian worldview offers an alternative, holding forth the promise of Jesus Christ of eternal life to those who follow him in this short earthly life. The Christian worldview has an explanation for death and is triumphant over it.

Fourth, the secular worldview breaks down in that it fails to take into account or to understand spirituality or transcendence. There is something in men and women that senses or feels there is something outside of themselves, bigger than themselves. There is something in men and women that has a sense of the spiritual and transcendent. There is something in men and women that wonders why there is so little love in the world and so much hate, or at best indifference.

The Christian worldview gives an answer that continues to attract people. The intellectuals and powerful reject the Christian worldview, satisfied that they have the answer in their superior minds or material goods. The poor all over the world hear the call of Jesus Christ to his personhood. For 2000 years, the Church has been in the world, however imperfectly, defectively, and badly, offering an alternative to power, greed, mammon, and lust. The Christian worldview, even if we say we cannot accept its truth because it asks too much of us to accept what we cannot see as actual facts, continues to attract people on a worldwide basis and has done so for over 2000 years.

The Christian worldview is not an ideology, is not a fad, is not a fashion, is not a philosophy, but is a person, Jesus of Nazareth. It is that person and his claim, that calls us all into question.

17. A Word about "Forgiveness"

"Forgiveness" is a significant and basic aspect of the Christian ethic. As a matter of simple fact, Jesus, in his model prayer, says the following in Matthew 6, verses 9-16,

> After this manner therefore pray ye: Our Father which art in heaven, Hallowed be thy name. Thy kingdom come. They will be done on earth, as it is in heaven. Give us this day our daily bread. And forgive us our debts, as we forgive our debtors. And lead us not into temptation but deliver us from evil: For thine is the kingdom, and the power, and the glory, for ever. Amend. But if ye forgive not men their trespasses, neither will your Father forgive your trespasses.

Forgiveness, in this model prayer of Jesus, is recommended to us with the statement that we should forgive our debts, a word that has also been translated as trespasses, as we forgive our debtors, or those who trespass against us. In verse 14, Jesus says that if we forgive men their trespasses, God will forgive us, but, on the other hand, if we do not forgive our fellow man their trespasses, neither will God forgive us our trespasses. The question is, what is forgiveness and why should we do it?

It is something of a conundrum, if not a riddle or mystery, that we should forgive those who damage us and hurt us. After all, the human reaction to having pain put upon us by another is to take revenge or, better put, return the favor. This command to forgive one who hurts us is puzzling since it goes against the basic grain of human nature, which "wants to get even." Be that as it may, the first question is, What is forgiveness?

Is forgiveness an excuse or saying I'm sorry? I think not. When one says excuse me, or excuses another, one puts the slight or offense aside, in a sense. To excuse is to let it pass. I do not think forgiveness is excusing. Nor do I think that forgiveness is forgetting. To forget is to not remember, or let it pass from our minds, as if it never happened. Forgetting is memory erasure or memory loss of an event, or slight, or pain inflicted upon us that, after all, might not be so easily forgotten.

Forgiveness is neither excusing nor forgetting. It is an internal act, emotional, spiritual, and intellectual of understanding the pain inflicted upon us and returning it with an attitude of love and understanding. Forgiveness of another who has hurt us is understanding that other person, and accepting, and apprehending their action against us, taking it into account and saying, I understand. Forgiveness is not forgetting. It is spiritually canceling out the pain and hurt that has been inflicted upon us.

The second question is, now that we have some understanding of what forgiveness is, is why do it? Jesus says that God forgives us our shortcomings, our failings, and our deficiencies, and the pain that we inflict on Him by our indifference and rejection of his Commandments and His love. He tells us that since God forgives us, we should forgive one another. That seems a good enough reason, but I think there is a more practical reason. The practical reason is that if we harbor, and let fester, the pain and the hurt that has been put upon us by others, we poison and ruin our own lives. To forgive is to grow. To not forgive and to hold onto pain and hurt is ultimately to hurt ourselves, more than we can ever hurt that other person. The price of holding onto pain and lashing out against the person that has given us that pain, is a far greater and higher price to pay than forgiveness.

In the practical sense, unless we forgive on a constant basis, every slight, every pain, and every hurt that others may intentionally, or even unwittingly, inflict on us, our lives will be a constant misery of poison subjectivism and self-involvement. Constant forgiveness lets us constantly grow in love towards one another. Our lives, without forgiveness, become impossible.

In short, I would say, that as in all other parts and aspects of the Christian ethic, the Christian life is the practical life. The alternative to loving your neighbor, is being indifferent, if not hating your neighbor. The command to love our neighbor is a practical command enabling us to get through life. I suggest, as with forgiveness, there is little or no alternative.

18. Salvation and Sacrifice: Comments on Some Concepts

The Biblical or Christian concepts or ideas of salvation and sacrifice are foreign to the modern world, which tells us through television and the media that everyone is happy and o.k., everyone is nice, and everyone is basically good. In short, modern man sees no necessity for salvation, since he sees nothing to be saved from. In a world that is all glitz and toothy smiles, the idea of salvation or of man being in need of repair, help, or reconstruction, is off base to most so-called advanced thinking men and women.

The Biblical perspective, or rather the Christian perspective, says that men are not so good, says in fact that they are corrupt, twisted, limited, degraded, and thoroughly lacking. The Christian faith and the Christian worldview says God has intervened in history in the person of his only begotten son to set things right, or to create a relationship with the Holy and Perfect God. The Christian faith says that men are not so great, and in fact, they are signally deficient in basic character and motivations.

The need for salvation is reasonably obvious to any thinking person. The fact of the matter is the world is rather a mess, and sad to say, is basically ruled by evil and Satanic forces. A glance at the daily newspaper reveals a current genocide in Darfur; constant death and murder in the Middle East; and other equally horrific events and stories. Those reports are the tip of the dark iceberg of human nature. We do not know, and this is probably fortunate, what goes on behind closed doors in every marriage; nor do we know that people have slipped from life into death, with no one caring or giving a damn. The best that can be said of most people is that they are largely indifferent to others and can be alienated and hostile if crossed.

The idea of salvation, therefore, is quite a reasonable notion and idea. The world has been a horror show for some time, and continues to be so. In the 20th Century, there have been a number of genocides, which other countries and people have largely done nothing to stop, whether the Turks in Armenia, the Jews in Europe and Germany, the Cambodians under Pol Pot, the Rwandans, and most recently the massacres and killings in Darfur. It is quite clear and obvious that salvation is a reasonable idea and offers a reasonable solution to correct a misdirected and failed human nature.

Second, the idea of sacrifice is foreign to the modern world. It must be said that our ancestors engaged in animal sacrifice, and sometimes human sacrifice, in an attempt to understand the world and propitiate powerful forces. They did not know whether the rain would come to grow the food, whether there would be enough water, and in short, whether they would survive in an uncertain and fragile world. Our ancestors did not have the scientific worldview and so did not understand what was going on, or whether they would live on to the next day disease free and pain free.

The modern world speaks little of sacrifice and sees no necessity for it, since we now believe we control nature, and through science have come to understand natural events and the ongoing process of life. Nevertheless, Christianity posits that sacrifice is necessary and absolutely necessary. God sees humankind as failed. He did not wish us to be failed, but we fell away from him into sin, selfishness, and self-love. The Christian faith argues that God, as a God of justice, had to sacrifice himself in the person of his only begotten son, Jesus Christ, to correct the deficit and deficiency in human nature and set us right, and into right relationship with God, the Creator and Redeemer of mankind.

I think Christianity correct in the idea of sacrifice. A woman who chooses motherhood engages in a great sacrifice, subsuming her needs and self to the needs of her children. The father who chooses to support these children chooses to sacrifice equally so. The scientist who spends long hours in his laboratory and, like Jonas Salk, has discovered a cure for polio has sacrificed his life to do something good for others. Doctors who go on medical missions to poor countries also engage in a financial and personal sacrifice. Without sacrifice, there is no growth and there is no love.

It is the extent of God's love that he would send his own being, in the person of his son to sacrifice himself out of his undying mercy and love for every person and every generation past, present, and future.

I think the concepts of salvation and sacrifice reasonable ones. They explain the world because the world needs repair and salvation, and this repair and making whole can only occur through sacrifice. It is only when we, even in our short and poor human persons and lives, sacrifice ourselves to the needs of others that we become fully human and attain salvation and rightness with God. I find the modern world distressing, and frankly, slightly ridiculous. The world of sitcoms, e-mails, and the quick-fix hardly explain the mystery of life. Salvation and sacrifice offer us great truth, and we fail to grasp these ideas and concepts at our great peril.

19. The One Way to God

Jesus of Nazareth, in his earthly life, said much of what, for want of a better word, might be termed of a radical, or even cryptic character. The Gospel of John contains a number of these sayings that at first glance are puzzling, if not shocking. Most people have a general conception of the deity or God in the modern world, given the number of religions, including Islam, Hinduism, Confucianism, and Buddhism. There would seem to be many paths to knowing God. Many people believe that they could know God through nature or through other people. This is not to say that these things are not true, or have some truth. Religious expression, in its manifold variety and nature, can lead us to know God in a certain sense. This is also true of our relationships with other people, or with the beauties of the arts, such as music, painting, and literature. Surely the arts represent a kind of spiritual expression that can lead us to the face of God.

Jesus, in the Gospel of John, presents quite a different picture concerning the issue of how we may come to know God. Jesus says that we can only come to know God through and by means of him. For example in John 10:9, Jesus says, "I am the door; by me if any man entering, he should be saved, and shall go in and out, and find pasture." In John 9:5, Jesus again makes the outrageous claim that, "As long as I am in the world, I am the light of the world." In John 11:25, once again we are faced with an even more apparently ridiculous and insane claim, when Jesus says, "I am the resurrection, and the life; he that believeth in me, though he were dead, yet shall he live." John 15:1 is another radical saying of Jesus Christ. Here he says, "I am the true vine and my father is the husbandman." In John 6:51, Jesus makes the simple, yet again radical, claim ,"I am the living bread, which came down from heaven; if any man eat of this bread, he shall live forever: and the bread that I will give is my flesh, which I will give for the life of the world." In that same chapter in verse 35, again Jesus says the same when he says, "I am the bread of life: he that cometh to me shall never hunger; he that believeth on me shall never thirst." Earlier in the Gospel of John, in Chapter 4:14, Jesus says, "Whosoever drinketh of the water that I shall give him, shall never thirst; but the water that I shall give him shall be in him a well of water springing up into everlasting life."

It seems that Jesus never ceases to make what appears to be a one way street for humanity concerning himself. He leaves us no options. He leaves us no way out. He says he is it, and this is it. Make your choice, and take your chances. He seems to say, it is me or nothing. To my knowledge, no human being in history has made such an apparently radical, if not insane, claim about himself.

In John 8:12, Jesus says, "I am the light of the world, he that followeth me shall not walk in darkness, but shall have the light of life." Finally, in the 14th Chapter of John, verse 6, the disciple John reports Jesus as saying, "I am the way, the truth, and the life: no man cometh onto the Father, but by me."

What can we paltry, weak, and fairly ineffective and corrupt human beings say of these sayings? The first question is did he say them? Since the Gospel of John has been in public circulation for some 2000 years, it would appear to carry some weight in human history.

Jesus said a lot of things. No one but he has ever said that he is the only way to know God and nobody else matters. This is the essential claim of the Christian religion. It is the historical claim, it is a truth claim. For some 2,000 years, Jesus of Nazareth has stood at the crossroads of history. Christianity, in the person and claim of Jesus Christ, brought the Roman Empire to its feet. Most lately, in Eastern Europe, Communism yielded before the Vicar of Christ. Communism in Russia promulgated atheism in trying to crush the Church. Jesus and the Church have risen up in that country. Jesus is a puzzling man. He makes us uncomfortable. He calls all of us into question. The fact of the matter is, he says I am it, it is me alone. This is the Christian claim. This is the Christian religion. The world waters it down. The world says all religions are the same, all people are the same, and everything and everybody, whatever their beliefs, have validity.

Jesus rejects the world system, and he calls us to him saying I am the only way, there is no other. The Church has been promulgating this message about this person, and what he said, for 2,000 years. We will see what will happen in eons and ages to come about him, about what he has claimed and what he has said.

20. The Compassion of Christ

I speak in this essay, not of the Passion of Jesus Christ, but of his compassion. His passion, his sacrificial life, death, and resurrection are separate items. Within his life and death, he offers us moral guidance, and redemption and the repair of a broken and twisted relationship with God, offering us new and eternal life. Little has been spoken of, or rather not enough of, his compassion.

Compassion is an elusive word and quality. We, as human beings, often speak of love, of being in love, or of being loved. Rarely is there discussion of compassion. Jesus, I think, offers some insight into what constitutes the quality of compassion. I think compassion may be defined as entering into other peoples' pain and suffering and taking it or apprehending it to your own self and humanity. Compassion involves not only entering into other peoples' feelings but, as it were, feeling those feelings. Perhaps compassion may be defined by the word empathy, rather than sympathy, since empathy is the quality of entering into other peoples' lives and their concerns and taking them to yourself and part of yourself.

Jesus, in some sense, is the epitome of what we can understand as compassion. At the end of his life, the evangelist Saint Luke records Jesus as saying, (Luke 23:43) to one of the thieves crucified beside him on the day of his death, "Verily I say unto thee, today shalt thou be with me in paradise." The Apostle Luke, in that same chapter (Luke 23:34), records Jesus as saying of his malefactors, crucifiers, and executioners, "Father forgive them; for they know not what they do." There is another incident that comes to mind that shows Jesus' compassion. Mary is said to come to Jesus and fall at his feet, saying to him, "Lord, if thou has been here, my brother had not died" (John 11:32). John records Jesus as seeing Mary weeping and the Jews also weeping who came with her, and John states, "He groaned in the spirit, and was troubled" (John 11:33). In John 11:34, Jesus asks, "where have ye laid him? They said unto him, Lord come and see," and in verse 35 it is said, "Jesus wept." The compassion of Christ is seen here boldly and starkly. It is not said that Jesus cries in self-pity, but weeps for the brother of Mary, who is dying and then deceased.

The compassion of Jesus, therefore, is all encompassing and all embracing. To his killers, he asks God to forgive them. To the basest of criminals, a thief, and one of the underclass and an outcast of society, he pronounces that that miscreant will be with him that day in paradise. For a broken, failed, corrupt, twisted, and empty humanity, he weeps.

The compassion of Christ is beyond human understanding. Most of us, in our relationships with people, offer little more than a few words of sympathy. For most of us, our lives are spent in self-thought, if not self-worship. The compassion of Christ moves all of us beyond this limitation and brings us into a full compassion that few of us are able to attain.

On the day that others give us pain, can we forgive them? Better put, when we are murdered, at the moment of our death, can we forgive our murderers?

Can we, in this materialistic and corruptly class-ridden world, based on wealth and power, equate ourselves with a criminal and thief, and say to him, you will be with me in paradise?

Most of us would not even talk to a criminal, and certainly not invite them to our homes to dine. The compassion of Christ reaches beyond human comprehension and understanding. It is entering into others, understanding others, being with others, and even suffering with others their pains and their lot, however dark and dank in life.

It comes to my mind that the contemporaries of Jesus were shocked at his behavior patterns. Each time I see people who adhere to class consciousness, wealth criteria, intellect criteria, or whatever criteria they may chose to use to uplift themselves, I recall this criticism of Jesus of Nazareth, frequently said in the Gospels, and recorded many times. In Luke 7:34, the Pharisees said of Jesus, "The son of man has come eating and drinking, and ye say, behold a gluttonous man, and a winebibber, a friend of publicans and sinners." Further, the evangelist Matthew records Jesus as saying that many publicans and sinners sat down with Jesus and his disciples and the Pharisees seeing this said to his disciples, "Why eateth your master with publicans and sinners?" See also Mark 2:16 and Luke 5:30.

Jesus' compassion reaches to the societal lowest of the low and basest of the base. Jesus' compassion knows no class or race distinctions. It is all embracing, offered and given to all, regardless of their false societal status that the world imposes on them. The compassion of Christ is not human compassion. It is the image of God's compassion that we are called upon to follow, as best we can.

21. The Image of God and Christ, or the Image of God and Christ in Man

This little essay, or literary excursus, will consider the concept of "image." The word image conjures up a flat, lifeless representation, such as a photograph, computer videogame, television program, or a movie. I intend to discuss, in this little work, Jesus as an image of God.

Firstly, I happen to believe that Jesus was and is God, or better put, that God revealed himself in Jesus and Jesus still lives in eternity and in communion with God the Father and the Holy Spirit, as the second person of the Trinity. For human beings, Jesus' life as recorded in the Gospels is a kind of image of who and what God is, and who and the kind of people we should be. Jesus evinced and revealed certain behavior patterns and characteristics in his life.

I find it significant that Jesus was not respecter of persons. He shocked his contemporaries by associating with, and I dislike using this terminology, lower class people. The Pharisees and religiously important people of his time could not understand why an educated Jewish man would choose to consort and socialize with the underclass. After all, most of us, frankly, not only look down on those people, but perhaps dislike them. Probably, to put it more bluntly, middle and upper class people in society feel superior to lower class people. Jesus, apparently, failed to share this point of view, but found value in many different sorts of people and in many different kinds of people, including criminals, tax collectors, and, as the Gospels use the word, sinners. It is clear that Jesus, as God, and we may be safe to say in assuming this, has no class consciousness.

Second, Jesus lived a life of service. He, apparently, did not earn a lot of money. He spent a life of loving, giving, and service. He cured people with physical illnesses and those cures are recorded in the Gospels as miracles, or miraculous cures. He lived a life of love and compassion. He had a particular love for children, whom he told us, we should be like, and people who were ill and hurt, emotionally and physically. He told all kinds of stories called parables to tell us what God was like and what we should be like. He told us that the important thing was to love God and to love our neighbor as ourselves.

I find it significant and, frankly, shocking that on the day of his crucifixion and execution, Jesus forgave one of the criminals beside him and told him that he would be with him that day in paradise. As well, Jesus asked God the Father to forgive his persecutors and torturers and executioners, saying that they did not know what they were doing.

I think Jesus gives us an image of what God is like, compassionate, caring, forgiving, humble, and certainly no respecter of persons. By the same token, Jesus, as a human being, gives us the image of what we should be as human beings. Jesus' life and work, therefore, give us two different kinds of images, one, the image of God's nature, loving, caring, in short, a nature of unconditional love, and, what we, as human beings, since he was a human being, are able to share in that image. Images are likenesses and replicas. Jesus is not a replica, a likeness, a photograph, or a portrait. He is the image of the living God's nature and the image of perfected human nature in all its infinite intellectual and personal possibilities.

22. The Idea of the Supernatural, or Religion vs. Science and Technologyy

Up until the beginning of the 19th Century, most of the Western world adopted a Christian worldview. That is to say, they believed that their actions in this earthly life would possibly bring them, through faith in Jesus Christ, to eternal life in heaven, or in the alternative, should they fail as human beings in these respects, eternal punishment in hell.

Perhaps it might be more accurately stated that the Christian worldview of another supernatural realm, existing parallel and above this earthly realm, had its last heyday in the 17th Century. For example, John Bunyan's *Pilgrim's Progress*; the poems and sermons of John Donne; the poetry of George Herbert; and most significant, the great epic poem in English, *Paradise Lost* by John Milton reflect this perspective and emphasis. In the course of the 18th and 19th Centuries, the Christian worldview of another world, and of our actions in this world earning our place in another world, have been gradually eradicated. The first expression of this eradication, and the end of society's consensus in this respect, was the Enlightenment in the 18th Century in Europe. With the advent and progress in science and technology in the 19th and 20th Centuries, at least in the Western world, the Christian "setup" of the world, consisting of hell, heaven, and earth has lost its hold on many people.

It should be noted that, surprisingly, despite the Enlightenment and the growth and development of science and technology, many people still have religious beliefs. This has surprised many academics, and perhaps politicians and businessmen, who are either too intellectual, too proud, or too pragmatic to see the point of religious belief. Nevertheless, throughout the world, and even in Western Europe and the United States, there are many profoundly religious people.

For many people, however, science and technology, and as it were, material progress, have weakened the hold of religion, and in particular, Christianity, on many elements of the population, particularly the wealthier and more educated classes, but even the middle classes. Religion, it would appear, in whatever form it may take, may seem to have a greater appeal to the poor and more disadvantaged groups in society. This should come as no surprise, since Jesus of Nazareth, even in his own time, attracted mainly the lower caste elements in his own society, or to put it bluntly, the poor people, who saw in him hope for equality, respect, and the hope of being valued and raised up within a system, which as is true in most systems, excluded and denigrated the poverty stricken.

I propose to comment on the idea of the supernatural and on whether it still has validity in this era where science and technology hold sway. The benefits of science and technology are obvious. In many ways this is the best and greatest time to live. Because of advances in medicine, people live longer and healthier lives. In 1900, in the Western world, the age span, on the average, was 40. In 1940, the end date was about 60. People now live more frequently to their seventies, eighties, and even nineties. Technology and science offer a better and more available world. Whereas people were confined at one time to their neighborhoods, they can now easily, and at a cheap price, travel all over the world and see the world. More is available. Almost everyone in the United States owns a car and has a computer.

In short, the enjoyment of life, and the availability of many material goods, have markedly increased and improved for most people. For many people, having even a house, one hundred years ago, was not even an option. Nowadays, with computers people can establish relationships with whomever they may choose and regard as likeminded all over the world. Because of science and technology, race and religion prejudices are no longer as available options, since the world has become more interconnected and globalized because of science and technology. The status of women, who are now independent, has probably improved for the better, since material prosperity for them has resulted in less confinement to the home and household drudgery.

In short, the world is quite a better world for science and technology, and life has improved for many, if not most, people. The question is, is religion and the idea of another world irrelevant?

I think not. As a starting point, the world is an extremely evil place, riddled with corruption. Human beings regularly kill and torture each other and ignore other people's needs, confining themselves to their own selfish little worlds and trying to get as much for themselves as possible in contradistinction to the needs of less fortunate individuals. The world, one might say, is a jungle, in which the strongest get the most and the best, and the weakest are left behind. Also, everyone dies, sometimes with a period of prolonged pain and suffering. I do not think men are all bad, and there is good in them, but for most people, life is a struggle to survive, and because of that, the world is a panorama of people scrambling for as much as they can get, and, to that extent, elbowing out in the process most other people. Moreover, there are questions as to how we all got here, where we are going, and literally what life is all about. Are we just brute animals or something more? Does this life end as unpleasantly as we came into it, live in it and finally die in it?

I think science and technology, although on a temporary basis they have done much for people, offer no ultimate answers or solutions to the questions I am raising. Yes, religious belief has been abused by twisted, corrupted, and degraded human nature to obtain power over the people. Nevertheless, all in all, I have to say that religion, and in particular Christianity, tries to offer a few answers to ultimate questions that perplex most people, if thought about. Unfortunately, most of us are too busy surviving to give much though to ultimate life questions. Religion, and in particular, Christianity, provides a few answers. It posits that the world is corrupt and mankind a fallen species, encased, for want of a better word, in sin. It says that this situation may not continue if, basically, we raise ourselves up, in our human nature. It says that we are not just beasts of the jungle, but something more, and we have a destiny beyond our animal natures. Despite the world being a completely confused place, there is support for a spiritual realm. Certain gifted individuals create beauty, whether in literature, music, or the plastic arts, sculpture or painting. Certain people provide extremely fruitful ideas that serve to remake civilization and make it better for all of us.

(By the way, I think ideas are the moving force in society, not power and money.)

Power and money follow ideas, rather than make them. Karl Marx sat in a library writing *The Communist Manifesto* and brought about the rise of Communism and the Russian Revolution. Adam Smith wrote the *Wealth of Nations* and brought about a capitalistic economic system which people are adhering to and following to this day. The idea is the creator and leader, the people who adopt it are the followers, whatever power they may attain to or hold.

Let me end this essay by saying, although science and technology have made a better world for us all, unfortunately they offer no ultimate answers. There is no man alive who will not see death, there is no man alive who will not suffer in their lives, whether at the hands of impersonal external forces such as disease or, sad to say, at the hands of their neighbors in their jobs and marriages. I would also add that love is a scarce commodity, unfortunately, in this present world. Everyone wants it, but nobody has time to give too much of it. In short, the world is an extremely fractured, deficient, and broken and twisted place. Religion offers an answer that, despite all this, we are something more, and can be something more. It is this proposal and idea that religion and Christianity offer to this. I, for one, happen to think that there is something beyond the material, and agree with the religious worldview that ultimately if we are not spiritual, we are nothing.

23. Freedom vs. Slavery

In the modern world, the word freedom has acquired, what I believe to be, a mistaken meaning and import. Freedom, in the world today, is interpreted as meaning that, as long as you do not break the law, you should be free to do anything you want. Implied and implicit in this notion of freedom, which many people embrace whole heartedly, is the idea that there are no fixed moral laws. Since we should be free, under this understanding of the concept of freedom, to do whatever we want, as long as we do not break any laws, one can only conclude that any objective morality has gone by the way side, to be replaced by a kind of moral relativism, which means that we make our own morality when we adopt this idea of freedom.

Under this understanding of the idea of freedom is the notion that we should be free to pursue whatever may please us at any given moment, as long as no one else is harmed, and one can only conclude that we can even be free to harm ourselves, if we wish, short of suicide. Thus, there has come about a kind of free market sexuality, embracing all kinds and types of sexual conduct, with the exception of incest, although some people will not even stop at that, if they can get away with it.

Freedom also, under this definition, involves pursuing and acquiring as many material goods as we can get and obtain. It involves and allows for a kind of excessive ambition with the result that life becomes a competitive race, where we all seek to outdo each other and make the others surrounding us potential rivals and enemies in pursuit of the material and power goal.

I have two arguments with this concept of freedom. First, I do not think to do exactly what you want, in the unfettered fashion that this word suggests in the modern world, results in any kind of freedom in the true sense. The freedom the modern world embraces, which most people think to be a good thing, results in a kind of self-worship, self-adulation, and certainly intense self-involvement.

The result is that rather than involving ourselves in positive and fruitful relationships of service and love with others, we shrink within ourselves, devoting ourselves to ourselves. The end is that we are somehow so self-encased as to be immovable and virtually helpless and nonfunctional. We are barely able to include others within the range of our concerns, and in so limiting and devoting ourselves to ourselves, we become virtually chained and encased within and to ourselves.

This is hardly freedom.

Freedom, properly understood, makes us involved outside of ourselves in love, service, and relationships with others. The freedom to do exactly what you want, leads to an increasingly shrunken personality and, if you will, soul. We become not grownup men and women, but remain petulant, selfish children.

Second, I do not think the freedom the modern world so lauds and praises brings us any happiness. Happiness consists of going outside ourselves. Happiness involves involvement with others. Happiness is relationships, and if you will, the basis for all relationships, friendship. When we have relationships, we step outside of ourselves. When we are free to do what we want, we are stricken, encased, and paralyzed in our freedom to do completely and exactly what we want.

I often have occasion to speak with elderly people, or not so elderly people, who for one reason or another, cannot work anymore. They say they are happier working and were happier working. Control and discipline and involvement in others, ideas, and tasks outside of ourselves bring us true freedom. The freedom to do what we want only brings intense self-involvement and great unhappiness. There could be no more unhappy person than a person who is alone, and free to do exactly what they want at the beginning, middle, and conclusion of each day of their lives.

Let me add this note, perhaps somewhat philosophical, but I think rather true. Freedom is embracing the good. Freedom to do what can be casually termed the wrong thing is no freedom at all, but only a privation. Evil has an impermanent existence; tyrannies rise and fall; imperialism gave way to democracy; kings gave way to Parliaments; apartheid gave way to self-government; and slavery and serfdom gave way to freedom. As long as we embrace selfishness and dominance in the guise of class advancement, we remain markedly and totally and completely unfree. Freedom with this many choices only leads to extinguishment and nothingness. There is only true freedom in love and service and involvement in the lives of others.

24. Creeds or Chaos?

The Christian religion, in its authentic historical form, is, for want of a better word, a creedal religion. This means that Christians agree, based on certain creeds, as to what it means to be a believing Christian. There are three ancient creeds. They are the Apostles Creed, which dates from the 8th Century and is a revision of the so-called old Roman Creed which had currency in the West by the 3rd Century A.D. Behind the old Roman Creed are relationships with forms in the New Testament itself. The Apostles Creed is so-called because its roots are Apostolic.[7]

The core of the Apostles Creed seems to be some sort of Baptismal formula.[8] It is beyond the scope of this literary excursus to go into the origins of the Apostles Creed on which many books have been written.

The second of the ancient creeds is the Nicene Creed, which was formulated, in part, in response to the Arian heresy. Arius maintained that the son had a beginning, but that God is without beginning and that the son is not a part of God. Arius believed he was protesting against what he believed to be the Sabellianism of his Bishop Alexander, who taught that God is always, the son is always, and the son is unbegotten begotten. In response to this controversy and dispute, the Emperor Constantine called a council that met in Nicea in Asia Minor in the year 325 A.D. The result of this council was the formulation of the Nicene Creed.[9] Again, it is beyond the scope of this little chapter to analyze the historical origins and history that led to the formation of the Nicene Creed.[10] The basic element of the Nicene Creed that is significant is the addition of the word "homoousion,," which means that Christ is of one substance with God the Father.

The third of the ancient creeds is the Athanasian Creed.[11] The Athanasian Creed has been ascribed to the Church Father Athanasius. For many Christians, as well as many other people today, these ancient creedal formulations, defining the basic dogma of the Christian faith, are either irrelevant, uninteresting, passé, or have been superseded. To many people the Greek philosophical terminology and background, which these creedal formulations make use of, is seen as outworn and irrelevant.

I have given the title Creeds or Chaos? to this chapter, because I believe that without these creeds the Christian faith is in chaos. At the present time, for many Christians, the Christian religion has been "watered down" to some general love feast. The creeds say the opposite. They posit a world structure, world vision, and belief system that goes far beyond some sort of shallow politics. They are metaphysical, philosophical statements of what is real, what is true, what life is all about, what we are about, and where we are tending and going. They give us a two-tiered vision of the world, which God in heaven reigns over mankind on earth in communion with the Holy Spirit and his only begotten son, Jesus Christ, risen from the dead.

The creeds offer us philosophical certainty and make claims of absolute truth. Without creeds, the Christian faith has no meanings. It is at the mercy of every fashion, fad, and temporary historical development that may come and go. The creeds tell us what the world structure is and what life is all about. Without creeds, the Christian faith and religion is left to the subjective interpretation of individuals who are unknowing, prejudiced, and often swayed by their own peculiar agenda.

I am refreshed in reading and reciting the creeds. They tell me of a life that is beyond the grave, of a God who will return, of a God who is threefold in persons, remaining one substance. They tell me that Jesus was born of a virgin, rose from the dead, and established his Church that will never die. The creeds plant us firmly in the ground and will outlive every fashion, every temporary fad, and every media show with which we are continually assaulted and propagandized. The alternative to the creeds is intellectual chaos. Without them, Christian and non-Christian will always be lost in a jungle of competing philosophic systems, based on human subjective perception, and often containing more error than truth. I am always stimulated in reading the creeds, since they take me out of my parochial present to eternity and truth.

25. Orthodoxy

Some years ago, the English writer G.K. Chesterton wrote a little book called *Orthodoxy*, in which he traced his journey to, what he referred to as, the Orthodox Christian faith. I'd like to talk a bit here about "orthodoxy," in the context of what it means to be a Christian in today's world. In the world today, orthodoxy is a bad word for many people, because it implies absolute truth, definitive truth claims, and a whole host of tenets with which the modern politically correct world is uncomfortable.

For many Christians today, ever since the Enlightenment in the 18th the Orthodox Christian faith has been seriously, "watered down." For many Christians, the confusion is so great that they are willing to believe that some sort of generalized love and tolerance constitutes Christian religious belief. That stance, in my opinion, is misconceived and incorrect. For that reason, I would like to say a few words about Orthodoxy or the deposit of faith.

Orthodoxy, or the Orthodox Christian belief system, for a starting point, presumes a number of principles. The first one is the existence of an omnipotent, omniscient, creator God, living apart from nature. The second principle is the idea that there is another world beyond our present material world. The third principle is that God created the world and mankind, and did so out of his love and his desire to share his Being with men and women, his created children. The fourth principle is that God reveals himself initially, in the Hebrew Bible through a series of historical events, including the handing down of the Ten Commandments on Mount Sinai, his covenant with the Jewish people, that still is in force to this day, his further revelation in the words of the prophets in the Hebrew Bible, and other historical events that are too numerous to delineate. The fifth principle of Christian Orthodoxy is that the Bible is the revealed word of God and at least one of the ways in which we come to know and understand God.

There are other principles in connection with Christian Orthodoxy, including God's revelation in Jesus of Nazareth, the Virgin birth, the miracles of the

New Testament, Jesus' death for our sins on the cross, his resurrection from the dead, and his ascension into heaven. The sixth important principle of Christian Orthodoxy is that the sacrifice of Christ was necessary on the cross to rescue us from sin and possible destruction, and, in a word, to repair our broken relationship with God, the creator.

The seventh principle of the Christian Orthodoxy is that God exists in three-fold form, being one substance and three persons, the Father, the Son, and the Holy Spirit. The eighth tenet Christian Orthodoxy is that by faith in Jesus we may obtain eternal life. There are other principles of Christian Orthodoxy including the sacraments such as Baptism and the Lord's Supper, by which we may obtain relationship with God and Christ and come to know God and Christ.

The ninth principle of Christian Orthodoxy is that Jesus will return again to judge mankind, some to eternal destruction in hell, and some to eternal life in heaven with him, and in this process will establish a new cosmic order.

This is a brief summary of what I believe is the Orthodox Christian faith. I am no astute theologian, nor terribly sophisticated in this area of thinking, but this much is clear, that the Christian dogmatic system is far more than a few loving words of encouragement, or some sort of politically correct tolerance in which the world tries to convince us that everybody and everything is ok. It is quite clear that things are not ok and the fact of the matter is, things are really very bad. Without laws, even in civilized Western countries such as the United States and the European countries, human nature, unloosed, would create an intolerable situation. In countries without laws, where strongmen rule, such as in Africa and Asia, life is basically impossible, and everyone suffers.

Human beings, far from being pleasant and nice, given the slightest smidgen of power are brutal and intolerable with respect to those whom they may perceive as under them. The simple fact of the matter is that the Christian dogmatic system posits a certain number of truth principles and makes a claim that we may choose to accept or reject at our peril.

I find the modern world's shallow, facile position, that things are getting better and better, and people are really very nice not true based on my experience. The Christian dogmatic system, or Orthodoxy, provides an explanation beyond the expectation and position of the modern world that people are really very nice. In fact, the world is a jungle in which the strong survive and the weak fall by the wayside and die. Christian Orthodoxy provides an explanation. I submit in this little essay that that explanation is far more reasonable than political correctness.

At the present time, the thought system of the world, I think it is fair to say, very shallow. For many people, materialism is as far as they wish to go, as establishing any life principles or having any thoughts beyond themselves. I find materialism unsatisfying and I do believe that anybody who adopts materialism as the answer is poverty stricken in imagination and intellect.

For all its faults or failings, Orthodoxy, to me, is the answer. It is clear that the world has been and always will be a mess at the hands of untrammeled human nature. Jesus provides a way out and offers an alternative, as Orthodoxy says. If you could find a better way of approaching the world, I am willing to listen, but at this point, nobody has thought up anything better or offered a better explanation with hope for the future.

26. *A Few Words about Evolution*

The so-called theory of evolution has acquired a kind of factual predicate in the scientific, academic, and even commonwealth communities. Not having read Charles Darwin's *Origin of Species* or *Voyage of the Beagle,* I approach this subject as basically ignorant. In that sense, I may be said to be hardly fit to make any sort of comment of an intelligent character on this significant historical landmark theory, which, since its articulation and inception, has acquired a kind of consensual truth by most of the world, or at least the western world.

Knowing so little of the details of Darwin's works and his theory, nevertheless, I choose here to make a few chance comments on my reaction to it, in short, its truth and validity. As far as I can glean, or figure out, Darwin's theory posits that by a process of natural selection and survival of the fittest, life developed from the sea into various species, including mammals. Apparently, Darwin opined or concluded that these changes are recorded in fossil remains and drew the conclusion that animals, fishes, mammals, and amphibians developed into various species, or better put gradations, over the course of thousands, if not millions of years.

Darwin eventually concluded, it would appear, that humankind has a connection with monkeys, gorillas, and the great apes. At first glance, he would appear to have a point. There is a similarity of appearance and continuity between people and monkeys. Monkeys appear to chatter, if not talk, quite a bit and move about in an upright position at times, as people do. It would seem they lack a rational faculty, as human beings do, but, nevertheless, there seems to be some sort of connection, I have to admit it.

The theory remains a theory, it must be said, since you cannot prove, or better put, you cannot exactly explain what gave rise to these various species, gradations, and kinds. All we know is, it happened. How it happened is a rather perplexing question. As a casual observer, having lived for some years, although that does not qualify me any more than anyone else, I have a number of problems with the theory.

The first thing is, why has it stopped. Why are new species of human beings, better, superior, stronger, if not possibly geniuses, coming into being? Darwin says this evolution occurred over a large period of time, and I have a confusion as to why it is not going on now.

My second problem with this theory is how this all happened by accident. I am unaware of cells presently or at any time undergoing change to produce new kinds of beings. Frankly, the theory in this sense is absolutely outrageous. I cannot believe, however long the period of time involved, that new things come about by happenstance and not creation.

The third issue I have with the theory is, and this is connected with my second problem with the theory, I have never known of anything coming into being by accident. A tree requires a seed, a house requires a builder to erect it, a bicycle requires someone to build it, a car requires someone to put it together. How, on earth these fantastic new gradations of species came into being, without someone doing it, I fail to understand.

The fact of the matter is, nothing happens that way, in my experience. Every time I do something, I do it because I will it. When I do it, something happens because of it. I go to the store to buy food to prepare a meal, and I make the meal. I write an essay, because I go about doing it.

In sum and in short, evolution fails miserably in accounting for these changes, without some sort of creative intervention. The evolutionists regard the people who believe in God creating things as primitive and out of scientific court. To my mind the creation theory better accounts for the facts. Everyone knows that everything has a cause. In fact, causation is a very deep set element of the cosmos. I have found that when I cause or do something wrong, I get it thrown back in my face, and when I do something good, or at least long enough or consistently enough, either nothing bad happens to me, or something good happens to me. The evolutionists find no causes. I find, in life, everything has a cause, a result, as an end.

The evolutionists, frankly, make fun of people who adhere or believe in the biblical account of creation in seven days. I do not, because I know in my experience that everything is created, from a sandwich to a gothic cathedral. For all I know, it might have happened in seven days. It certainly is closer to the truth than saying people emerged from the fishes.

This is my last word about evolution, or last few cursory superficial comments on the subject. The best thing that can be said of it is that it is nothing more than a theory, and the worst that can be said of it is that it miserable and ineluctably fails to explain or account for both the facts and normative and normal human experience. I conclude this little essay by saying that the intelligentsia makes fun of so-called fundamentalists. I think the reverse is true. I think the fundamentalists better account for the facts and the evolutionists are grasping at straws. It stretches human rational thinking beyond belief to think that anything came out of the sea and began to walk around, no matter how much time elapsed. It is also an insult to my intelligence to believe that I descended from an orangutan or a monkey. That is my opinion for all its worth. I note at the end of this little work that there is a world beyond western secular society, in which the vast majority of humankind still believes in God. A few proud convinced moderns have decided they know better. I do not believe they know anything, as much as I think I do not know anything, or rather I do not know enough, but I know this much, that nothing happens without a reason or cause and an ending.

27. A Little Light on Intellect, Intelligence, or Being Smart

In the modern world, intelligence, intellect, IQ, academic intelligence, or being smart for many people, if not most, have a premium value. Our society is a competitive one and puts great emphasis on intellectual and academic ability. We admire people who are smart, and often many of us, if not most of us, have the desire to be smarter or brighter than the others around us.

The simple reason for this is that in the past men, and to a lesser extent women, accomplished their ends by brute force. Cavemen used their brute strength to vanquish their neighbors, enemies, or adversaries. For many centuries this was the most frequent scenario in society, that is to say, men took what they could get, whether wives, land, goods, or whatever else, by brute strength. It should be noted that the class structures in society, even in the modern world, have their genesis in particular families' having acquired more wealth, goods, and land than others, at some point in the past, thereby becoming upper class, and by that method attaining economic superiority, if not economic subjugation, over their immediate neighbors, who in this process and devolution became lower class.

Intelligence and brains, academic ability, and being smarter than other people have replaced brute strength as a method of obtaining power, wealth, goods, position, and status in society. As a result of this, the modern world requires many years of schooling, and puts a premium on those individuals who have the requisite academic talent to obtain, by this method, upper class status. As an aside, academic talent is only one form of intelligence and intellectual ability, and it is an incorrect emphasis that the modern world places on this particular species of talent. Surely, there are other forms of talent and ability, which include creative ability, business ability, athletic ability, and for the wife and mother, nurturing and caring ability.

In any event, as a convinced Christian, I must differ from this emphasis on "smartness." Being smart, or better put smart or intellectual, is not the main thing is life, nor is it the only personal or character quality that is worthy or worthwhile. Paul the Apostle, the greatest of philosophical and religious thinkers in the history of the world in my opinion, has a different view. St. Paul presents a different perspective on the premium the modern world puts on intelligence, intellectual ability, or whatever might be contained under this particular rubric. In his letter to the Corinthian church, Chapter 13, he says the following:

> If I speak in the tongues of men and of angels, but have not love, I am a noisy gong or a clanging cymbal. And if I have prophetic powers, and understand all mysteries and all knowledge, and if I have all faith, so as to remove mountains, but have not love, I am nothing. If I give away all I have, and if I deliver my body to be burned, but have not love, I gain nothing.
>
> Love is patient and kind; love is not jealous or boastful; it is not arrogant or rude. Love does not insist on its own way; it is not irritable or resentful; it

does not rejoice at wrong, but rejoices in the right. Love bears all things, believes all things, hopes all things, endures all things.

Love never ends; as for prophecy, it will pass away; as for tongues, they will cease; as for knowledge, it will pass away. For our knowledge is imperfect and our prophecy is imperfect; but when the perfect comes, the imperfect will pass away. When I was a child, I spoke lie a child, I thought like a child, I reasoned like a child; when I became a man, I have up childish ways. For now we see in a mirror dimly, but then face to face. Now I know in part; then I shall understand fully, even as I have been fully understood. So faith, hope, love abide, these three; but the greatest of these is love.

It is clear that, for the Apostle to the Gentiles, love is greater than fancy speech or, rather, the speech of angels. Prophecy, mysteries, knowledge, and the faith to move mountains, and material goods are nothing, for the Apostle Paul, in comparison with the quality of love, or what might be better understood as charity. He says that when he was a child he spoke like a child, reasoned like a child, and thought like a child, but when he became a man he gave up childish things, which include all those things that he had enumerated as nothing in comparison to charity or love. He says that of the three qualities of faith, hope, and love, the greatest of these is love.

For the Christian and for St. Paul, knowledge, intellect, arrogant intellectual superiority, or the desire to be smarter or better than others is nothing and negative in comparison with love and charity. For the Christian, love is the aim, not being smart or smarter, or if we look to the past, being brutal, brutish, and stronger than our neighbors. It is love and charity that build a better world, not surface, facile smartness. It is smart and the ultimate aim to be kind and loving. It is stupid to be smarter than others when the aim is stamping those around us intellectually under our feet.

A final note, I have always found it ironic and significant that Jesus chose as his disciples and apostles, not the richest and not the smartest, but simple working folk-fishermen. To these seemingly not so smart people he entrusted the salvation of the world.

28. Who Were the Disciples?

This little essay will concern itself with talking about the Disciples of Jesus Christ, and a little bit about Jesus Christ. This first must be said, that apart from being an itinerant preacher and healer, Jesus was a carpenter. Thus, in the thirteenth chapter of Matthew in the 54th and 55th verses, certain individuals are reported as saying of Jesus "where did this man get this wisdom and these mighty works? Is not this the carpenter's son?" Clearly, the contemporaries of Jesus were quite astounded that a carpenter could be so wise and intellectually piercing.

Let us take this a little further. In the Gospel of Matthew, the fourth chapter, verses 18-22, Jesus is represented as asking Simon Peter and his brother Andrew, who were fishermen, to follow him and he says to them that he will make them fishers of men. Further, in verse 20, Simon Peter and Andrew are said to have left their nets and followed Christ, and then in verse 21, when Jesus sees two other brothers, James, the son of Zebedee and John his brother in the boat with Zebedee their father mending their nets, he calls them to be his disciples. Clearly, Jesus, a working man, was choosing working men as his disciples, in this case, four fishermen: Peter, Andrew, James, and John.

In the ninth chapter of Matthew, verse nine, Jesus is represented as calling Matthew, a tax collector, as his disciple. Similarly, the Gospel of Mark, chapter one, verse sixteen, tells of Jesus calling Peter, Andrew, James, and John—all fishermen—to be his disciples, and Matthew in chapter two, verse thirteen, a tax collector, also as his disciple. Certainly a tax collector is not a very glorified or glorious occupation. In fact, in the second chapter of Mark, verse fifteen, Jesus is represented as sitting at his house with many tax collectors and sinners, along with his disciples. The scribes and Pharisees were astounded that he was eating with sinners and tax collectors and said to his disciples, "Why does he eat with tax collectors and sinners?" (Mark 2, verse 16). Clearly, the educated elite of that society of Palestine in that day were astounded and could not understand that an educated Rabbi, if not clergyman, could spend his time with what they perceived as the dregs of society.

Similarly, in the Gospel of Luke, Chapter five, verses 8-10, Jesus is represented as calling as his disciples Simon Peter, Andrew, James and John. In the fifth chapter of Matthew, the 27th verse, Jesus is represented as calling his disciple Matthew, or Levi, the tax collector. Again in the Gospel of John, the first chapter, Andrew and Simon Peter are called as Jesus' disciples by him.

Obviously, however one may view Jesus, whether as the Son of God or merely a great religious and ethical leader who founded a religion that has endured to this day, and gains converts on a daily basis throughout the world, it is somewhat puzzling that he himself was a working man, that is to say a carpenter, and that he chose as his followers, if not friends, workingmen, fishermen and a tax collector, one that society, in that day, despised as unworthy and the agent of the Roman emperor. One may wonder why this compelling personality and great intellect chose to be a working man and chose as his followers and friends workingmen.

As I have indicated in this little piece of work, Jesus' educated contemporaries were puzzled, if not astounded, that he could consort with these kinds of people. The world in its present manifestation emphasizes money as the indicia of success and class status as the desiderata obtained by the accumulation of wealth. Although working people are not openly viewed with contempt, I would speculate that those of wealth and "class" do, in fact, despise working people as somewhat beneath them. Jesus had the great wisdom and insight to realize that working class people are quite as intelligent and prescient as educated people or wealthy people. One may only conclude that Jesus thought that working people were quite as worthy and intelligent as wealthy and educated people.

Finally, I would add one little thought here. Jesus chose as the agents of his gospel and grace, working people. One may safely conclude that Jesus' message will always have a greater appeal to the underclass, who suffer, than to the upper class who prosper. Jesus had the great intellect and psychological insight to realize that the gospel message falls much more aptly on the working people than on the privileged.

In short, he chose fishermen and a tax collector as the agents of his grace and love. For every atheist and secular person, there are ten thousand poor Hispanics, crowding a Pentecostal church. The proof of the pudding is in the eating.

29. A Few Words on the Commandment "Love Your Neighbor As Yourself"

In his teachings, Jesus of Nazareth said many things in many situations. One of his most thought provoking commandments is found in the Gospels of Matthew and Mark. The Disciple Matthew presents in Chapter 19, Jesus as saying, "Thou shall love thy neighbor as thyself." Again, in Chapter 22, verse 37-39, Jesus says, "Thou shalt love the Lord thy God with all thy heart, and with all thy soul, and with all thy mind" (verse 37). In verse 38, he says, "This is the first and great commandment," and in verse 39 he says, "and the second is like unto it thou shall love thy neighbor as thyself." In verse 40 of the twenty second Chapter of Matthew, Jesus was said to have noted, "On these two commandments, depend all the law and prophets."

The Evangelist Mark quotes Jesus as saying, in Chapter 12, verse 30, "Thou shalt love the Lord thy God with all thy heart, and with all thy soul, and with all thy mind, and with all they strength, this is the first commandment," and in verse 31, Jesus is quoted as saying, "and the second is like, namely this, thou shall love thy neighbor as thyself, there is none other commandment greater than these."

This short little essay proposes to examine certain aspects of Jesus' commandment to love our neighbor as ourselves. The commandment is somewhat puzzling at first glance, since we are told to love our neighbor as ourselves, and it would appear that Jesus is recommending that we love ourselves. Perhaps love of self has been incorrectly interpreted. Most probably the meaning of the saying is that we should treat our neighbor with the same respect and consideration, with which we regard ourselves.

The second observation about this commandment is, in fact, that it is a commandment. It would appear that the love of our neighbor does not come easily to us, and so it is commanded. Certainly, fallen human nature posits and involves self-love, and self-centeredness, as opposed to love of our neighbor, whom we may not know at all, be indifferent to, or not care about at all. Thus, the commandment, in its inception, is a difficult if not challenging command for human nature to fulfill. Nevertheless, it is commanded, and Christians who follow Christ are told that they must follow this commandment of showing charity and love to all who may pass us by in life. To love our neighbor as ourselves is perhaps impossibly difficult, and most people can only half-way do it or accomplish it.

The third and most shocking aspect of this commandment is that Jesus tells us to love our neighbor as ourselves, but he does not tell us that our neighbor will love us back. He merely tells us to do it, expecting nothing in return. Again, the commandment is most difficult to fulfill since most human beings look for reciprocity and connection in their relationships.

In sum, this is a commandment that we are taught to fulfill, and the irony of it is that as much as we may love our neighbor, there is a good, if not even ,chance that we will receive no love in return. This is the Gospel, and this is the commandment of the Savior and Redeemer of the world.

Notes

1.   Matthew Black and H.H. Rowley, eds., *Peake's Commentary on the Bible* (Nashville, Tenn.: Thomas Nelson & Sons, 1962), 410.

2.   C.S. Lewis, *Reflections on the Psalms* (New York: Harcourt, 1958), 2.

3.   All quotations and references to the Psalms are taken from the *Book of Common Prayer* (New York: Everyman's Library, 1999).

4 .   The Lord is my shepherd: therefore can I lack nothing.
      He shall feed me in a green pasture:
            and lead me forth beside the waters of comfort.
      He shall convert my soul: and bring me forth in the paths of righteousness,
            for his Name's sake.
      Yea, though I walk through the valley of the shadow of death,
      I will fear no evil: for thou art with me;
            thy rod and thy staff comfort me.
      Thou shalt prepare a table before me against them that trouble me:
            thou hast anointed my head with oil, and my cup shall be full
      But thy loving-kindness and mercy shall follow me all the days of my life:
            and I will dwell in the house of the Lord forever.

5.   Hold not thy tongue, O God of my praise:
      for the mouth of the ungodly, yea, the mouth of the deceitful is opened to me.
      And they have spoken against me with false tongues:
            they compassed me about also with words of hatred,
            and fought against me without a cause.
      For the love that I had unto them, lo, they take now my contrary part:
            but I give myself unto prayer.
      Thus have they rewarded me evil for good: and hatred for my good will.
      Set thou an ungodly man to be ruler over him:
            and let Satan stand at his right hand.

When sentence is given upon him, let him be condemned:
   and let his prayer be turned into sin.
Let his days be few: and let another take his office.
Let his children be fatherless: and his wife a widow.
Let his children be vagabonds, and beg their bread:
   let them seek it also out of desolate places.
Let the extortioner consume all that he hath:
   and let the stranger spoil his labour.
Let there be no man to pity him:
   nor to have compassion upon his fatherless children.
Let his posterity be destroyed:
   and in the next generation let his name be clean put out.
Let the wickedness of his fathers be had in remembrance in the sight of the
   Lord: and let not the sin of his mother be done away.
Let them always be before the Lord:
   that he may root out the memorial of them from off the earth.
And that, because his mind was not to do good:
   but persecuted the poor helpless man,
   that he might slay him that was vexed at the heart.
His delight was in cursing, and it shall happen unto him:
   he loved not blessing, therefore shall it be far from him.
He clothed himself with cursing, like as with a raiment:
   and it shall come into his bowels like water, and like oil into his
   bones.
Let it be unto him as the cloke that he hath upon him:
   and as the girdle that he is always girded withal.
Let it thus happen from the Lord unto mine enemies:
   and to those that speak evil against my soul.
But deal thou with me, O Lord God, according unto thy Name:
   for sweet is thy mercy.
O deliver me, for I am helpless and poor: and my heart is wounded within
   me.
I go hence like the shadow that departeth:
   and am driven away as the grasshopper.
My knees are weak through fasting:
   my flesh is dried up for want of fatness.
I became also a reproach unto them:
   they that looked upon me shaked their heads.
Help me, O Lord my God: O save me according to thy mercy.
And they shall know, how that this is thy hand:
   and that thou, Lord, hast done it.
Though they curse, yet bless thou:
   and let them be confounded that rise up against me;
   but let thy servant rejoice.
Let mine adversaries be clothed with shame:
   and let them cover themselves with their own confusion, as with a
   cloke.
As for me, I will give great thanks unto the Lord with my mouth:
   and praise him among the multitude.
For he shall stand at the right hand of the poor:

to save his soul from unrighteous judges

6.   For the idea behind this article, see C.S. Lewis, *The World's Last Night* (New York: Harcourt, 1960).

7.   I believe in God,
       the Father almighty, maker of heaven and earth:
       And In Jesus Christ, his only Son our Lord:
       who was conceived by the Holy Spirit, born of the virgin Mary,
       suffered under Pontius Pilate, was crucified, dead, and buried:
       he descended into hell, the third day he rose from the dead,
       he ascended into heaven,
       and is seated on the right hand of God, the Father almighty,
       whence he shall come to judge the living and the dead.
       I believe in the Holy Spirit, the holy Christian church,
       the communion of saints, the forgiveness of sins,
       the resurrection of the body, and the life everlasting.   Amen.

8.   For a discussion of the origins of the Apostles Creed see Kenneth Scott Letourette, *A History of Christianity*, Volume 1, Beginnings to 1500 (New York: Harper & Row, 1975), 135-36.

9.   I believe in one God,
       the Father almighty, maker of heaven and earth
       and of all things visible and invisible.
       And in one Lord Jesus Christ, the only-begotten Son of God,
       begotten of the Father before all ages, God of God, Light of Light,
       very God of very God, begotten not made,
       being of one substance with the Father,
       through whom all things were made:
       who for us men and for our salvation came down from heaven,
       was incarnate by the Holy Spirit of the virgin Mary, and was made man:
       who for us, too, was crucified under Pontius Pilate, suffered,
       and was buried:
       the third day he rose according to the Scriptures, ascended into heaven,
       and is seated on the right hand of the Father:
       he shall come again with glory to judge the living and the dead,
       and his kingdom shall have no end.
       And in the Holy Spirit, the lord and giver of life,
       who proceeds from the Father and the Son:
       who together with the Father and the Son is worshiped and glorified:
       who spoke by the prophets.
       And I believe one holy, Christian, and apostolic church.
       I acknowledge one Baptism from the remission of sins,
       and I look for the resurrection of the dead and the life of the age to come.
       Amen.

10.   Kenneth Scott Letourette, *A History of Christianity*, Volume 1, Beginnings to 1500 (New York: Harper & Row, 1975), 153-64.

11.   Whoever wishes to be saved must, above all else,
            hold the true Christian faith.
       Whoever does not keep it whole and undefiled
            will without doubt perish for eternity.
       This is the true Christian faith,
       that we worship one God in three persons and three persons in one God.

without confusing the persons or dividing the divine substance.
For the Father is one person,
the Son is another,
and the Holy Spirit is still another.
but there is one Godhead of the Father and of the Son
and of the Holy Spirit, equal in glory and coequal in majesty.
What the Father is, that is the Son and that is the Holy Spirit:
the Father is uncreated, the Son is uncreated, the Holy Spirit is uncreated;
the Father is unlimited, the Son is unlimited, the Holy Spirit is unlimited;
the Father is eternal, the Son is eternal, the Holy Spirit is eternal;
    and yet they are not three eternals but one eternal,
     just as there are not three who are uncreated and who are unlimited,
    but there is one who is uncreated and unlimited.
Likewise the Father is almighty,
the Son is almighty, the Holy Spirit is almighty,
    and yet there are not three who are almighty
    but there is one who is almighty.
So the Father is God, the Son is God, the Holy Spirit is God,
    and yet they are not three Gods but one God.
So the Father is Lord, the Son is Lord, the Holy Spirit is Lord,
    and yet they are not three Lords but one Lord.
For just as we are compelled by Christian truth
    to acknowledge each person
    by himself to be God and Lord,
so we are forbidden by the Christian religion to say
    that there are three Gods or three Lords.
The Father was neither made nor created nor begotten by anybody.
The Son was not made or created, but was begotten by the Father.
The Holy Spirit was not made or created or begotten,
    but proceeds from the Father and the Son.
Accordingly there is one Father and not three Fathers,
    one Son and not three Sons,
    one Holy Spirit and not three Holy Spirits.
And among these three persons none is before or after another,
    none is greater or less than another,
    but all three persons are coequal and coeternal,
and accordingly, as has been stated above,
three persons are to be worshiped in one Godhead
and one God is to be worshiped in three persons.
Whoever wishes to be saved must think thus about the Trinity.
It is also necessary for eternal salvation that one faithfully believe
that our Lord Jesus Christ became man,
for this is the right faith, that we believe and confess
    that our Lord Jesus Christ,
    the Son of God, is at once God and man:
    he is God, begotten before the ages of the substance of the Father,
    and he is man, born in the world of the substance of his mother,
    perfect God and perfect man, with reasonable soul and human flesh,
    equal to the Father with respect to his Godhead
    and inferior to the Father with respect to his manhood.

Although he is God and man, he is not two Christs but one Christ:
  one, that is to say, not by changing the Godhead into flesh
  but by taking on the humanity into God,
  one, indeed, not by confusion of substance
  but by unity in one person.
For just as the reasonable soul and the flesh are one man,
  so God and man are one Christ,
  who suffered for our salvation, descended into hell,
  rose from the dead,
  ascended into heaven, is seated on the right hand of the Father,
  whence he shall come to judge the living and the dead.
At his coming all men shall rise with their bodies
  and give an account of their own deeds.
  Those who have done good will enter eternal life,
  and those who had done evil will go into everlasting fire.
This is the true Christian faith.
Unless a man believe this firmly and faithfully, he cannot be saved.

Chapter 3
Essays on Politics and Law

Introduction

This group of essays or, as it were some of my reflections and thought, occupies the fields of politics and law. The first essay critiques the feminist movement and observes that feminism has its problems and limitations. I note in this essay that women should have an equality of opportunity, both in the private and public sectors, and I also note that women and men share the same essential human nature, and that there is little distinction or difference in their essential human personhood. I also note that many feminists through some essential erroneous train of thought or thinking caricature all men as tough, sharp, unfeeling, inconsiderate, and self-important, and adopt that caricature as the essential male sex. I observe that men and women share equal sensitivities and equal feelings. Second, I observe that the second philosophical mistake in feminism is that toughness, callousness, and lack of feeling are good qualities and are to be imitated. I conclude that a caring, kind person is the human desideratum regardless of that person's gender or sex.

The next essay, "Life or Death," considers the law as to whether the terminally ill patient has a right to die. This essay concerns the pertinent case law concerning the continuing medical treatment in the face of serious, if not terminal, illness. Next comes an analysis of "Politics and Truth," and I say in this essay that political jargon has replaced true analytical thinking and serves to obfuscate and hide the truth in our modern world.

In "Legalizing Prostitution," I argue against legalizing prostitution, since to legalize is to approve a tawdry, harsh, and hard relationship, and brings down the social level to nothing more than ugliness and degradation.

In the essay, "A Third Party Proposal," I argue that we have a need for a third party, since the Republican Party in its alliance with Evangelical protestants and the Roman Catholic Church on the issues of homosexual rights and abortion, using the guise and pretext of the traditional family and religious values, is constantly transferring wealth to a smaller and smaller minority of the American population, as well as the corporate sector and, in addition, the Republican Party is destroying and demoralizing the working class Americans by bringing in immigrant sweatshop labor, thereby depriving the American worker of the chance to be in the middle class. I also observe the Democratic Party, the party of the left since the days of Franklin Roosevelt, have identified themselves with the rights and concerns of the poor and minorities, when in fact, the United States is a relatively prosperous nation with the most opportunities for the disenfranchised. I say that the Democratic Party in its concern for the poor and minorities occupies the better moral ground, but in its concern to be identified with, for want of a better word, fringe groups whether feminists, homosexuals, agnostics, or atheists, at some unidentified point in time lost the loyalty and allegiance of the American middle class. I offer as a solution to this paradox a proposal for a third party which embraces the traditional family, but nevertheless addresses the concerns of the weak, marginalized, poor and oppressed.

The essay of "Why Capitalism is a Failed Idea" essentially posits the notion that capitalism is based on greed and power and, in that sense, is mistaken and erroneous in its philosophical underpinning. The "Interview with Rick Seymour" is a capsulated overview of the life and work of one of the leading Labor/Employment/Civil Rights lawyers in these times.

The essay "Trade, Profession, or Profit," recognizes that we as lawyers must support ourselves, as any group of workers must do. However, it reflects on the idea that materialism and self-enrichment are not values, and should not be values for one who seeks to render a caring and professional service. The essay "A Discourse on Equality" analyzes that people are not inherently equal in their talents and abilities, but are equal as citizens in the common wheal, and certainly are equal in the sight of God and therefore share spiritual equality.

The essay "Race and Class: False Standards in Search of an Answer" proposes the answer that race or class have no meaning and that the ideal society is classless and race blind. Finally, the concluding essay, "Universal Healthcare Now," suggests that money should not determine access to healthcare, and that any just society must provide for universal healthcare for all its citizens regardless of economic status, race, class, or whatever that person may be inherently or accidentally, and whatever position they may occupy in society. In short, I argue that health should not be a matter of wealth.

1. The Feminist Movement: A Critique

Feminism has its historical and philosophical basis, understanding, and under-pinning, in the notion that the patriarchal system of the past, whereby the male sex, whether husbands, heads of state, kings, counselors, or cardinals, subjugated the female sex to their purposes and ends. The husband supported his wife and family, providing both financial and emotional support; the head of state or king, and his male counselors, ran the kingdom; and the senators and representatives in the republic who voted or held office were only men.

The feminist movement proclaims an end to this subjugation and male superstructure that women claim was a method of men's gaining or dominating family leadership, holding the major offices of business and state, and even ruling the religious hierarchy.

Today, we have seen women as Prime Ministers in England, India, and Israel; being ordained as priests in the Anglican Church; and as Cabinet members and elected members of the Senate and House of Representatives in the United States.

Women feel, rightly so, that there should be equality of opportunity in the public and in corporate office, as well as in the professions and family, and that the old patriarchal system of societal domination by fathers, elder sons, husbands, and kings should end.

This writer has no argument with the obvious truth that men and women share the same human nature and are entitled to the full panoply of rights and opportunities as citizens of the republic and children of the omniscient God. There can be no argument that half the minds and potentialities of the human race should be limited and confined to household tasks and drudgery.

This writer, as I said, has no dispute with this quest for full equality and opportunity, but I do have an argument with the persona and image of sharpness and aggressiveness that the feminists adopt in their desire to be equal to and, I think they believe necessary, to compete effectively with the male dominant world.

It would appear that feminists feel or conclude that all men are tough, sharp, aggressive, unfeeling, inconsiderate, and self-important, and so they should be too. The feminists would seem to believe that, surrounded by our machismo society, they must become this to obtain full respect and equality. This particular persona and belief about the male sex, as a matter of right thinking, is mistaken. It is incorrect that all men share the personality of football players or Steve McQueen. The male sex, just as the female sex, can be nurturing, dependent, or even feminine, just as the female sex, depending on the woman, can be the aggressive and dominant factor in the relationship. Apparently, the feminists feel that this typical stereotypical personality image was the method by which the male sex obtained dominance over the physically weaker female, and that for women to gain equality and recognition this questionable quality must be adopted and imitated. All men are not tough and unfeeling, nor are all women kind and considerate. These qualities are equally distributed through both sexes.

In fact, speaking as a man, men in some respects may be more sensitive than women in some areas. It is safe to say that there are many men who wish to be fathers and nurturers as well as women who wish to be mothers.

It is significant, if not ironic, that the supposedly insensitive male species has produced the most sensitive love poetry, most stirring oratorios, and most beautiful works of art.

Second, there is a second philosophical mistake underpinning this desire for imitating this image of the cutting edge male. That is, that it is in fact a desirable quality. Even if toughness, callousness, and lack of feeling are traditionally male qualities, it is open to dispute whether they are worthy of imitation. These are qualities of the uncivilized, brute, and primitive, in a word, the qualities of less developed minds and personalities. Surely, these qualities are not to be imitated or desired. Clearly, I believe, the feminists are mistaken, first in assuming this is a male quality, and second adopting it at all as a personal quality.

More to the point, we all, men and women, are linked together whatever our religions or our age, in some sort of love and connection with one another. We all are together on a march to slow death. None of us is an island in him or herself. We are all part of the main, and every man and woman's death diminishes us in some respect. So said John Donne, the metaphysical poet and priest of the Anglican Communion. To imitate and essentially laud the stupidest and most violent and most cruel characteristics of the male nature is essentially to caricature in some way the male sex that has produced Buddha, Confucius, Jesus, Moses, Shakespeare, Milton, Dante, Handel, Bach, Virgil, and Homer.

To be tough, biting, and cruel is to stereotype the male sex in some sort of box, ignoring its caring and sensitive members for criminals and moral reprobates. In any event, I say, to be tough, unfeeling, and uncaring are totally undesirable qualities in anyone, man or woman, and not to be considered the object of adulation and imitation. The Feminist movement is good in that it argues for, and hopefully obtains, full equality and development for all members of the human race, regardless of their gender. It is mistaken if it adopts, as a male persona, the lowest and least desirable male qualities. To be tough, unfeeling, and without care is a personal and spiritual error that only serves to alienate people and repel them. These qualities are not male or female qualities, but negative qualities. Insofar, as a feminist adopts these qualities, as a desideratum, it is wrong. We, none of us, can reach our full human nature regardless of sex, race, or sexual orientation, without understanding that we all share human limitations, that we are all essentially weak vessels, and it is only through caring and sharing that we can bring about a better life for us all, men and women alike.

2. Life or Death

The question whether the terminally ill patient, suffering acutely and in dire pain, can choose to end his own life,—or whether the spouse or closest relative of that person can make that so—is a question that has been in the forefront of society in the past few years. Terri Schiavo's case was a example of this that was in the news for some years. In 1990, Terri Schiavo, then in her mid-twenties, suffered a cardiac event that produced a severe cerebral injury. Terri Schiavo entered into a coma in which she remained, albeit in an impaired state of consciousness, for fifteen years. Her family continued to think that she had modest signs of awareness of her surroundings, but in the end her husband acquired a different view, losing hope of any further recovery. In the end, after a series of court battles, her husband's right of guardianship was upheld and the gastric tube removed, food and drink forbidden by Court Order, and within some two weeks Ms. Schiavo perished.

In many parts of the world this would be an unimportant, unnoticed, and unheralded and virtually non-controversial event. The phenomena of death in most of the world where dire poverty rules is little noticed or taken account of. We in the United States have embraced an ethic that places value on human life, whether mentally impaired or physically limited in some fashion, for better or for worse.

It is the purpose of this article to examine the current state of law in the State of New York with respect to the issue of the right of the terminally ill patient to choose death or of his guardian or closest relative or spouse to do so for him.

The leading and seminal case is *Cruzan v. Director, Missouri Department of Health.*[1] In *Cruzan*, the Petitioner sustained severe injuries in an automobile accident and was thereafter confined to a Missouri state hospital in a persistent vegetative state in which she exhibited motor reflexes, but no indication of significant mental functioning. The hospital employees refused, without Court approval, to honor the request of her parents to terminate her artificial nutrition and hydration, since that would result in death. A state trial court authorized the termination, holding that a person in Ms. Cruzan's condition has a fundamental Constitutional right to direct or refuse the withdrawal of death-prolonging procedures. The Court further noted that Ms. Cruzan had expressed to a former housemate that she would not wish to continue her life if sick or injured unless she could live a normal life, which to the court had suggested that she would not wish to continue on with her nutrition and hydration. The State Supreme Court reversed, holding that the right to refuse treatment was not applicable in this case. The court further stated that the State Constitution did not include within it a broad range of privacy that would support an unrestricted right to refuse treatment and that there was a doubt that the Federal Constitution embodied such a right. The Court decided that the State Living Will Statute included a state policy strongly favoring the preservation of life and that Ms. Cruzan's statements to her housemate were unreliable in terms of determining her intent. The Court rejected the argument that Ms. Cruzan's parents were entitled to order the termination of her medical treatment, concluding that no person could assume that choice for an incompetent in the absence of the formalities required by the Living Will Statute or clear and convincing evidence of the patient's wishes.

The Supreme Court of the United States held that the United States Constitution did not forbid Missouri from requiring that clear and convincing evidence be proved of an incompetent's wishes as to the withdrawal of life-sustaining treatment. The Court held, however, that a competent person has a liberty interest under the Due Process Clause in refusing unwanted medical treatment, but added that the question of whether that Constitutional right has been violated must be determined by balancing the liberty interest against relevant state interest. The Court concluded that the State Supreme Court did not commit Constitutional error in concluding that the evidence adduced at trial did not amount to clear and convincing evidence of the patient's desire to cease hydration and nutrition and that due process did not require the state to accept this substituted judgment of close family members absent substantial proof that their views reflected those of the patient.

Thus, the United States Supreme Court held in *Cruzan* that the common law right to refuse medical treatment was a Constitutional interest under the Due Process Clause.

The Court of Appeals of the State of New York in the matter of *Eichner v. Denis Dillon*[2] faced a similar set of facts. In *Eichner*, two cases were before the Court of Appeals, *Matter of Eichner* and *Matter of Storar*. In *Matter of Eichner*, Brother Fox, an 83-year-old member of a religious order was being maintained by a respirator in a permanent vegetative state. The local director of the society applied to have the respirator removed on the ground that it was against the patient's wishes as expressed prior to his becoming incompetent. In *Matter of Storar*, a state official applied for permission to administer blood transfusions to a profoundly retarded 52-year-old man with terminal cancer of the bladder. The patient's mother, also his legal guardian, refused consent on the ground that the transfusions would only prolong his discomfort and would be against his wishes if he were competent.

In each of these cases the Court below found that the measures should be discontinued. Both patients, however, died. The Court concluded in *Eichner*, once again, that a competent adult has a common law right to accept or decline medical treatment. In *Eichner*, the Court held that it was proper to discontinue the patient on the respirator on which he was being maintained in a permanent vegetative state where the patient prior to becoming incompetent had consistently expressed his views not to have his life prolonged by medical means if there was no hope for recovery. Thus, the Court again held that the Court below had properly approved discontinuance of Mr. Eichner on the respirator at the request of the patient's guardian.

Matter of Christopher[3] is also relevant on this issue. In *Christopher*, the hospital petitioned for authorization to perform a procedure, percutaneous endoscopic gastrotomy, which was basically the surgical insertion of a feeding tube into the stomach and intestines of an elderly hospital patient. The Supreme Court of Queens County held that clear and convincing evidence existed showing that use of artificial means to prolong the patient's life was against her wishes and would be futile and unnecessary.

More exactly, the Court reasoned that New York, as well as most states, recognizes the common-law right of a competent person to decline medical treatment. The difficulty, however, the Court stated was the fact that the patient was totally incompetent and would never be able to express her wishes regarding the use of the feeding tube. The Court said the standard here was that the patient's wishes should be ascertained by and must be established by clear and convincing evidence.

Citing *Matter of Eichner*, the Queens County Supreme Court held that the application to use this feeding tube for the patient should be denied since there was clear and convincing evidence that the use of artificial means to preserve her life was against her wishes.

Again, the Court in *Christopher* reiterated the law that the terminally ill patient has the right to refuse or decline medical treatment to unnecessarily and futilely preserve his life.

Similarly, in *Wood v. Strong Memorial Hospital of the University of Rochester*,[4] the Appellate Division Fourth Department noted that competent adult hospital patients have the right to decline treatment and that although the state will act to prevent suicide, merely declining medical care, even essential treatment, is not considered a suicidal act or indication of incompetence. The court cited in support of this rule *Matter of Fosmire v. Nicoleau*.[5] Similarly in *Matter of Gordon*[6] the Supreme Court of Rockland County held that the right to refuse treatment exists in common law and is protected by the Due Process Clause of the New York State Constitution and that this right extends to mentally ill persons and to a voluntary patient in a mental hygiene facility. The Court noted that an individual must have the final say in decisions regarding his medical treatment to ensure that the greatest possible protection is accorded his autonomy and freedom from unwanted interference with the furtherance of his own desires.

Finally, in *Matter of Rosa M.*[7] the Supreme Court of New York County considered the case of a Director of a Psychiatric Hospital who applied for an order authorizing administration of electroconvulsive therapy to an involuntarily committed patient. The Court held that the patient was competent when she signed in writing her clearly revocation of her consent to ECT, and thus the hospital could not continue to give ECT even if the patient was not currently competent to make medical decisions. The Court held specifically that the fundamental right of individuals to have the final say in respect to decisions regarding their medical treatment extends with equal force to mentally ill persons who are not to be treated as persons of lesser status or dignity because of their illness.[8]

Conclusion

This brief review of some pertinent case law concerning the continuance of treatment in the face of serious, if not terminal, illness reveals a basic and over-riding rule in this State. Namely, that if the patient's wishes can be precisely and exactly ascertained, then the patient has the right to refuse treatment for whatever reason, even if death should be the result and should ensue. There is the argument that some quality of life, whatever slight, is of value; that recovery is always possible; and that love crosses all corners and barriers of incompetence and dying. Nevertheless, balancing the interests, the Courts of this State have determined that the individual's wishes are paramount and that medical treatment can be refused and that direction carried out, even when incompetence has taken hold, as long as the prior wishes of the individual can be known and ascertained.[9]

Reprinted by the permission of the Queens County Bar Association, Queens Bar Bulletin, *November 2005, Vol. 69, No. 2*

3. Politics and Truth

At the present time, we are barraged, if not bombarded, with what, for want of a better word, may be termed propaganda. Most of what assaults us through and by the media are subtle, if not outright, lies, and have no truth.

Unfortunately, the danger exists of confusing truth with political sloganeering.

Former President Bush said he wished to make citizens of illegal aliens, mostly Hispanic. This seeming act of good will, if not charity, serves to undermine severely the American worker's ability to earn a living and support his family at a sufficient wage. Thus, the former President's apparent purpose is not to aid the many illegals in this country, who have no business here in the first place other than to provide cheap labor, the purpose of which is to enrich corporate America's coffers.

Former President Bush, as did former President Reagan, endorses supply side economics. They posited that by not taxing the wealthiest sectors of society and the most profitable businesses, jobs will be created and trickle down to the workers of America. Supply side economics, again, is nothing more than a political slogan, and is really a lie, since its real purpose is to enrich the rich and make them richer.

Former President Bush offered faith-based charitable initiatives to displace government social programs by private charity. In truth, he wishes to remove the government from medical care and social welfare, and remove the social safety net by transferring these programs to private charity, leaving the poor, aged, and disadvantaged without the basic social safety net they so desperately need.

Former President Bush promoted deregulation and at the same time polluted the environment. He promoted laissez-faire capitalism as an idea and philosophic system, i.e. materialism, when it is nothing more than an economic system, sad to say, based on greed, selfishness, ruthless competition, survival of the fittest, and self-aggrandizement.

In short, political propaganda and sloganeering have no truth in them.

The Democratic Party says that they are the party of the poor. Yet we all know America is a relatively rich industrialized country with some poor, but surely not poor in the sense that a person from South America, Asia, or Africa might be so said to be.

Politics and political hype are not to be confused with truth. The truth is that as private citizens we should be charitable to our neighbors, yet we all must recognize the need for the governmental safety net. The truth is capitalism has its points in offering people incentives and opportunities, but should and must be modified and controlled by social programs, such as Social Security, Medicare, Medicaid, the Minimum Wage, and Unemployment Insurance.

The truth is that class distinctions, which are the result of economic dominance and subjugation by some fortunate few, are the product of human arrogance, evil, selfishness, and should be eliminated as much as possible to equalize our society. The truth is that cheap labor attacks the American workers' ability to get jobs and hold them. The truth is that enriching industry through deregulation is wrong, since future generations' ability to enjoy our natural environment is severely compromised. The truth is that homosexual marriage is possibly not a good thing, but, on the other hand, homosexuals are citizens and entitled to equal rights and equal treatment under the law.

The truth is supply side economics, another lie, may create a few jobs, but under the guise of that terminology, the wealthiest sectors pay no taxes and far from trickling down the money, hold it for themselves. The truth is that although we are told that selfishness, greed, and materialism are good things, and will make us happy, we surely know that as human qualities and ideas they are not good, and do not make people happy.

Where then can we find truth amidst this rain of media lying? This is a hard question and the answer is equally hard. The fact is that nothing can replace the Christian worldview, the Bible, or the great ideas in Western civilization. More important, nothing, amidst this cacophony of untruths that are forced on us, should compromise our ability to critically think and sort. It is only through our own reflection, in the course of our lives, along with our exposure to the great ideas of the past, that we can understand our world and ourselves. We will never understand sadism, cruelty, egotism, and selfishness, without understanding that men are, on some level, corrupt and blackened in their souls.

We will never understand that materialism is not the answer, until we recognize that men and women have a spiritual nature, that they will live beyond the grave, and that all our lives will come to an end, perhaps sooner than we think.

We will never understand the world or be surprised at it, until we recognize that men have corrupted and debased a good thing.

Politics, political propaganda, and sloganeering are nothing more than artful lies serving to deceive and obfuscate true life principles that we all must find in the course of our lives, and that we may be acute enough to see and grasp as they are presented to us and offered to us.

4. Legalizing Prostitution

There is a movement afoot that prostitution, illegal in most western and non-western societies, be made legal. The idea is that the crime is victimless, harmless and better controlled in specific districts under state and medical supervision.

The fallacy is twofold. First, those who frequent prostitutes, for whatever reason whether for sex, variety of act, or out of the isolation and loneliness characteristic of capitalist and western society, most truly harm themselves. Using another for lust without love is to harm the innards and is the denigration of a relationship that should be founded in community and intimacy.

The fact that no one is hurt facially does not change the hardness and tawdriness accompanying prostitution.

Second, even if it could be argued that prostitution has no victim and that no harm is done, nevertheless the idea falls short. Certain crimes, though apparently of antique origin exist not so much to penalize, but to assure that a certain social level is maintained. To legalize prostitution because it will occur in any event, whether legal or not, is to give the imprimatur, and even respect, to something that though done and done frequently should not be approved.

To legalize is to approve. To approve is to encourage. To encourage is to open the gates to the plethora of apparently victimless criminal activity that if allowed diminishes and denigrates us all.

Illegal prostitution is a finger in the dyke. The flood is better stayed.

5. A Third Party Proposal

The American two party system is in confusion and disarray. The Republican Party presents itself as the party of traditional values, or more simply put, family values. The Republicans claim an alliance with traditional heterosexual marriage and the nonworking wife. Within, and implied in, this particular political appeal is a rejection of the homosexual minority and feminism or feminists. The Republicans have also allied themselves with the forces of Protestant Fundamentalism, with its emphasis on personal salvation and having a personal relationship with Jesus Christ. The Republican religious alliance is with the fundamentalist churches, nondenominational, Baptist and Pentecostal, bypassing, if not rejecting, the mainline Protestant churches, such as the Methodist, Episcopalians, Congregationalists, and Presbyterians.

The Republicans also ally themselves with the Roman Catholic Church on the basis of that Church's opposition to abortion.

A product of this alliance with the Protestant Fundamentalists and, to some extent with the Roman Catholic Church, is the Republican party's selective moral agenda, focusing on opposition to abortion and homosexual marriage.

Under the guise and pretext of its embrace of traditional family and religious values is a constant and continuing transfer of wealth to a smaller and smaller minority of the American population, as well as to the corporate sector.

A consequence of this support of corporate America and the wealthy 1% is a gross and massive outsourcing of jobs to third-world countries such as India, China, Korea, and Taiwan, where cheap, if not sweat-shop, labor does the work at 1% of the wages of the formally unionized American worker, who is left unemployed and without transferable job skills.

In the meantime, there is a continuing flow of immigrants to the United States, mainly Hispanic, who do the work at 1/10 the price that the formerly unionized American worker was paid.

Thus, under the guise of support for the traditional family and for traditional marriage, there is an immoral concentration of wealth in fewer and fewer hands, and the pauperization of the American middle and lower-middle class, depriving these citizens of the opportunity to obtain stable quality employment and so enable them to support their families.

The Democratic party is the party of the left and since the days of Franklin Delano Roosevelt has identified themselves with the rights and concerns of the poor and disaffected, in particular concerning themselves with the rights of minorities including Black, Hispanic, Third-World immigrants, and women.

Since the United States is a relatively prosperous, for the most part, if not advanced country, the quasi-socialism and social action emphasis of the Democratic Party falls somewhat flat.

In some sense, the Democratic Party in its purported concern for the poor, and its desire to bring the marginalized minorities into the political and economic mainstream, occupies the better moral turf.

Unfortunately, the Democratic Party in its desire and concern to be identified with what, for want of a better word, may be called fringe groups, whether feminists, homosexuals, transsexuals, agnostics, or atheists, at some unidentified point in time lost the loyalty and allegiance of the American middle class.

What then can we say? What is the solution to this moral paradox, where one party embraces sexual morality, while the other identifies itself with social needs, charity, and concern for those who lack advantages and opportunities.

I propose a third party, which embraces the traditional family, but nevertheless sees the need to care and provide for the weak, marginalized, and oppressed. In this way, the totality of moral concern is addressed with the encouragement and acceptance of stable family life, along with the a social concern that leaves no one out and gives everyone, Black, Hispanic, immigrant, feminist, and atheist—in short the have nots—an equal chance and, if necessary, a step up. This is my proposal for a new Third Party.

6. Why Capitalism Is a Failed Idea

The capitalist system posits a free market place based on competition. The idea behind it is that each person is given an equal chance, and an equal starting point, to better and advance themselves, economically or in any way they choose and desire. The capitalist system is an economic system. It is not a political system, and most certainly not a philosophical or religious system.

The core basis of capitalism is that competition and the desire for money and material goods, or better put greed, provide the best chances and the most opportunities for the majority of persons to better themselves and their families.

In its basic form, capitalism is grossly and unduly harsh, giving the greatest rewards to the strongest and leaving the weaker elements of society to fend as best they can, or even die, whether those weaker elements are the old, the disabled, or the mentally dysfunctional.

Since the capitalist system is based on competitiveness, greed, or more aptly put the survival of the fittest, it fails to some extent even as an economic system, since those "who cannot make it," lacking the genetic basis to do so or lacking sufficient funds, must fail to avail themselves of any opportunities the system may offer and are left behind to lead their insufferable lives.

In sum, the result is that a large percentage of the people, in this harshest of systems, have no or little chance, due to its ruthlessly competitive character, pitting each person against the other.

More significantly, this system fails as a political system and most certainly as a philosophic idea.

Any political system should set out to provide some degree of equality and even sharing for its members. Capitalism rewards brute strength and some degree of ruthlessness in its participants. It makes the acquisition of material wealth the sole good and desideratum, shoving and pushing aside other values such as, as I stated, sharing and equality. It most certainly rejects any notion of charity and love and concern for others as possessing any validity. As an idea and political construct, it is intellectually bankrupt, based as it is on greed and animal competitiveness, and rewarding aggressiveness and degrading any concept of giving and contributing.

In many ways socialism, though also a failed idea and political system, is closer to the ideal society we should all wish to obtain as persons. Unfortunately, socialism, in its operation, in depriving its citizens of any incentive and opportunity to advance themselves whether materially or otherwise, also fails.

In its idea of redistributing wealth, sharing, and providing for all to some degree regardless of their wealth, class, intellect, or advantages, it is superior.

The answer may be a measure of both systems. What then can we say? Capitalism as a political or philosophic system has no particular meaning. In this sense it is vacant and vacuous.

Any person is totally poverty stricken in intellect, imagination, or spirit who places getting things for themselves above humane and human concerns.

Socialism makes us all into automated workers. The participants in any system must and should be given the chance to advance and develop themselves to their full capacity, even to the exclusion of others. In this sense, socialism fails miserably.

The best system is the system that provides the fullest and fairest opportunities to all its citizens regardless of race, class, sex, or wealth, allowing and permitting each of us to develop to our full potential and, withal, providing for the weak, poor, and disadvantaged, giving help to all, seeking in every respect to ameliorate the suffering and pain that at some time must come to us all.

7. An Interview with Rick Seymour

When I was asked by Steve Bierig of the Labor and Employment Section of the ABA to interview Rick Seymour, who has contributed so much to the field of employment discrimination and class-action litigation, I approached my task with great hesitation, knowing of Rick's monumental accomplishments in the field.

This interview cannot adequately describe Rick as a person, or his professional contributions, significant beyond belief. Rick told me that the motivating force in his life is to bring justice, fairness, equality and constitutional protection to all those who he may chance to service in his professional work.

Rick graduated from Harvard Law School in 1968, and was then admitted to the District of Columbia Bar that year.

Since October 1, 1969, Rick has specialized in the litigation of large-scale employment discrimination class actions. His experience with these cases began in 1966, when he worked as a law student summer intern placed by the Law Students Civil Rights Research Council at the New Orleans office of the Lawyers' Constitutional Defense Committee. When Rick graduated from Harvard Law School in 1968, he then worked for the next sixteen months as a staff attorney for the United States Commission on Civil Rights, and from October 1, 1969 until September 30, 1973, was an attorney with a Washington Research Project, Inc., a civil rights organization that sponsored fair employment litigation and other civil rights litigation. Rick left the Project on October 1, 1973, and opened his own office, where he continued to spend approximately 95% of his time in class-action fair employment litigation. In January of 1977, he began working for the Lawyers' Committee for Civil Rights Under Law, a committee which was founded in 1963 by the leaders of the American Bar, at the request of President Kennedy, in order to help defend the civil rights of minorities and the poor.

In addition to its national office in Washington, D.C., the committee has had affiliates in Boston, Chicago, Denver, Los Angeles, Philadelphia, San Antonio, San Francisco, and Washington, D.C.

Its litigation docket included numerous civil rights cases across the country, including a large number of cases challenging discrimination in employment, voting, housing, or education, on the basis of race or sex. In February of 2001, Rick left the Lawyers' Committee and joined Lieff, Cabraser, Heimnann & Bernstein, LLP (LCHB) as a partner.

LCHB is a plaintiff's class-action firm headquartered in San Francisco, with offices in New York, Nashville, and Washington. The firm handles numerous types of plaintiffs' class-action work, including employment discrimination, Fair Labor Standards Act cases, RICO, antitrust, securities fraud, product defects, and international human rights cases, including Holocaust cases. Since joining Lieff, Rick has been continuously working in and contributing to class-action litigation in the employment field. Rick has handled, to very successful conclusion, many class-actions cases where he has also made law.

I can only speak about a few of them that Rick suggested, and, in fact, he thought these were his most societally important cases enforcing the constitutional rights of minorities and the underprivileged. For example, the court in *Sledge v. J.P. Stevens & Co.*, 10 E.P.D. & 10, 585 (E.D.N.C. 1975), found class-wide discrimination in hiring, initial assignments, promotions, racial reservations of various job categories for whites, etc., in nine plants and three office facilities of the defendant, 12 E.P.D. & 11, 047 (E.D.N.C. 1976) (issuance of decree), 585 F.2d 625 (4th Cir. 1978), *cert. denied*, 440 U.S. 981 (1979).

Brewer and Miller Brewing Co., C.A. No. 93-CV-1600(FJS) (N.D.N.Y.), was a class action on behalf of 97 African-American employees and former employees challenging co-worker racial harassment against them through painting and posting racist graffiti and cartoons, the use of the plaint's public-address system to broadcast racial slurs and insults, and similar actions. The case was settled in 1995 for almost $2.7 million in compensatory damages. Again, Rick brought this class action to this very successful conclusion. Perhaps Rick's most important case was *Pegues v. Mississippi State Employment Service*, 488 F.Supp. 239 (N.D. Miss. 1980). This was a class action against MSES and against the Secretary of Labor challenging racial and sexual discrimination against blacks and women in employment referrals. The district court decided the case adversely to the plaintiffs. The Fifth Circuit affirmed in part and reversed in part, entering its own findings of class-wide racial and sexual discrimination to several MSES practices. 699 F.2d 760 (5th Cir.), *cert. denied*, 104 S. Ct. 482 (1984). On May 7, 1990, the Fifth Circuit rejected the MSES defendants' arguments against the award and reversed a limitation on the award. As a result of the appeal, the amount of the revised judgment entered nunc pro tunc as of October 14, 1988 and $4,787,905.83. With additional interest, the amount distributed to the plaintiffs and their class was $5,838,543.02. The decision was reported at 899 F.2d 1449 (5th Cir. 1990). Rick has been Co-Counsel also for plaintiffs in many other employment discrimination or civil rights actions and has been also co-counsel in the filing of numerous briefs in the Supreme Court on behalf of the Lawyers' Committee for Civil Rights under Law. In addition to the direct representation of plaintiff, Rick has for some years provided technical assistance and advice to attorneys handling fair employment cases against public and private employers for a variety of law schools and organizations, including the ABA; the National Employment Institute; and various public-interest organizations and Bar Associations. Rick has taught many training conferences for fair employment lawyers throughout the country and is a frequent speaker to groups of industrial psychologists. Rick was even invited as an "individual expert" and participant at an international conference on Namibia and Human Rights sponsored by the United Nations and held in Dakar, Senegal, in January of 1976, and was one of a number of American Civil Rights attorneys who spoke at a conference held in Oxford, England.

Rick has co-chaired committees of the Labor and Employment Sections of the many Bar Associations and in 1991, 1992, and 1993, co-taught a graduate level course in employment discrimination law as an adjunct professor at Georgetown University Law Center. On numerous occasions, to date, he has delivered or prepared congressional testimony on behalf of the Lawyers' Committee for Civil Rights under Law on questions involving Equal Rights Employment Opportunity and other Civil Rights questions.

Rick has authored law review articles, too many to list or even explain, and has written and co-authored a number of book chapters in the employment field. My interview with Rick took over one hour. I cannot adequately describe Rick as a person other than to say that Rick is a man of great modesty, charm and is self-effacing to a fault. His contributions have been great, and one can only say and hope that Rick, predictably, of course, will continue in his dedication to the legal profession and the class-action employment field, bringing justice, fairness, and equality for those, who by reason of their life circumstances, are unable to do so by their own efforts. We, as Rick's colleagues, express our congratulations and good wishes to Rick, who has done so much for so many.

Reprinted from the ADR in Labor and Employment Law Committee Newsletter, *Summer 2004*

8. Trade, Profession, or Profit

I taught a class on the basics of law geared to preparing students for competency in Paralegalism. A student remarked: "The best lawyers charge the most." I differed and countered that those who charge the most are the most greedy and, if you will, most avaricious, and not necessarily the most competent.

The student's remark reflected the current philosophy of the current age: rank, sordid, materialism. If our present society may be said to inculcate and promote any thought or valuation system, it is materialism: sex, self, gaining, getting, and outdoing."

We, as lawyers, must support ourselves as any group of workers must do. It follows, however, that the purpose of our profession is to render a competent professional service within the financial reach of as much of the general public as possible, and not to engage in a course of purely selfish self-aggrandizement to the end that we may acquire not a humble Ford, but a status Lexus, not a home in middle income Queens, but an estate in the Hamptons.

Materialism, self-enrichment or the simple raw acquisition of wealth is not a value system. Wealth acquisition is not a value. Honest, integrity, love and the desire to contribute to society, not take from it to enrich ourselves, are values.

A profession and a society that embraces materialism as a value must fail. We wonder why our society produces no poetry, no music other than a resounding glaring din, no drama, and no art, and yet we continue to embrace materialism, rejecting romance for pure animalism, and embracing cold secularism, turning away from any religious or spiritual life for power and money. We strip our youth of feeling and meaning, and bid the empty spiritual celibates be fruitful. We create a race of men without chests and women without hearts, embracing acquisitiveness as the answer. If we are to continue as professionals, and if our system and society are to continue to survive, we must recognize that materialism is no value, but must lead us to empty nothingness. Material goods equally distributed make a better life possible for us all and enable us to enjoy the higher goods and not devote our lives to sex and earning alone. The answer is in values beyond ourselves that will create and remake us. Materialism must fail because truly it does not lead even to happiness, but only to a fretful self-involvement. Most important, it must fail because it fails to recognize that we men and women are not flesh alone, but something more. Materialism must fail because it is simply not true and only leads to emptier and emptier lives, devoid of beauty, goodness, and truth. The material basis of life is a necessity, not an end. Actual goods are the basis for our participation in the higher goods, which permit us to grow. Without material goods we cannot survive. With them we move beyond the immediate necessities.

Materialism alone must bring only emotional and spiritual deprivation, cutting us off from love and being itself. Materialism is no value, but only a privation. It has been tried before. Communism brought in Capitalism; Imperialism, Independence; Aristocracy yielded to Democracy. Any system based on selfishness and materialism, values our society so fervently currently embraces, will and must die a slow death.

Reprinted by permission of the Queens Bar Association and the Queens Bar Bulletin *from Vol. 67, No. 8, May 2004*

9. A Discourse on Equality

American society, at the present time, and for some time, has had a passion for equality. This passion extends to the phrase, "everybody is the same." This phenomenon may, in a word, be defined as egalitarianism. There is a lot of good behind this passion for equality and the egalitarian character of American society, which posits and emphasizes that everyone be regarded as essentially equal, and given equal treatment as human beings, under the law. These little few words I am writing will attempt an analysis of what is meant by equality, or better put, understood by the word and term equality; will consider its desirability and deficits, if any; and will also attempt to analyze and examine the sources of equality.

Equality is basically a good thing. It is good that people be treated with equal respect, irrespective of their race, sex, appearance, wealth, intelligence, or class. It is also good that people be given equal chances and opportunities in society to obtain an education, to advance in the workplace, and to improve themselves materially, or in whatever way they may choose. A small minority of people may choose a life of service, as Mother Teresa chose. They are a thin sliver of the population, but that is their choice. They embrace a life of poverty and seek to serve the poor. For others, their choice is to advance themselves materially as much as possible. Others wish intellectual advancement, others physical advancement: they want to get stronger. A society which offers equal opportunity for all, in all categories and respects, is a good and advanced society and system. The issue is, what is the source of equality and what is meant by it. There are I think, two sources of equality, or the notion and idea of equality. There is political equality, the fact that in the United States, and in other countries with a parliamentary system, each person has an equal vote, from the billionaire to the pauper, from the illiterate to the writer of the Encyclopedia Britannica.

The idea behind political equality is twofold. First is the belief that the common man is not so common or lacking in insight and intelligence, as one might be led to believe. The core basis of political equality is a belief in the wisdom residing in the life experience and intellect of each and every person and citizen. Political equality also has its genesis in the idea that shared power and distributed power is better than concentrated and limited power. Power spread out among the entire voting electorate results in a better society than power concentrated in one person, which has historically given rise to tyrannies.

The second reason and understanding connected with and understood in the term equality, is spiritual equality. Spiritual equality posits that all men are created by God and are of equal value in the creator's eyes, again, irrespective of their wealth, looks, clothes, outward appearance, weight, wealth, class, or race. Both political equality and spiritual equality are true, but they have been wrongly extended, or in some sense extended too far, with the result that equality, as a word and concept, has lost its meaning, in some sense.

Political equality and spiritual equality do not mean that all men are equally gifted in their talents and abilities. There are outstanding classical musicians, outstanding writers, outstanding major league baseball players, and outstanding scientists. The persons who do not and cannot attain to these sorts of attainments and accomplishments in life cannot be said to be equal to those individuals who do. Of course, there may be reason for this disparity between the greats and the not so great. Perhaps some people have no wish to do that type of thing and would rather have an easier life. Their health may limit them. Their finances and economic status may limit their possibilities. When all is said and done, however, there are talented people, and not so talented people, and, I believe, that the talented people should be given credit and recognition and not be told that they are the same as everybody else. This may be said to be the great failing of a democratic society. Because of this passion for equality, equality's meaning has been stretched beyond what it actually means, in some sense. Equality does not eradicate quality. Equality should not result in the hammer being placed on every person who stands out. That person should not be told that the great effort he has made in achieving some little thing, is nothing.

Therefore, I propose, that the term equality be redefined in the three senses I have just suggested. Equality as human beings under God and in a democratic society does not come to mean equality of talents. I think it is a form of envy of the lesser talented to denigrate the achievements of the more talented. A startling beautiful woman may be told, because of envy and jealousy of other women, that she is not so beautiful and the people who say that may say that they are just as good in that respect. I think this passion for talent equality and achievement equality, or anything that makes one outstanding above another, is a form of envy and jealousy emanating from a root desire to say to yourself when you see another who has on some level surpassed you, I am as good as him.

How will I end this little literary product that I am creating? I end it by saying actual equality does not really exist and is not to be confused with political and spiritual equality. Political equality and spiritual equality, I suggest, should include the infinite variety of talents which may be found and can reside in each and every human being, and should, rather than hammering those talents in the name of egalitarianism, accept them, credit them, and reward them.

10. Race and Class: False Standards in Search of an Answer

The human race is divided into races, basically three in number, the darker races, the Asian races, and the Caucasian race. There is much hullabaloo about race in the world. Rationally analyzed and understood, race is no more than a species, genus or division of humankind. Race is no more significant than different kinds of monkeys, whether orangutans or African gorillas, or different kinds of dogs and horses. There should, in reality, be little or no discussion or issue about race, since it simply represents the variety of physical human nature and expression.

Yet throughout the ages, race has been an issue blown sky high and out of proportion, far out of relation to its actual significance. Let it be said here, that human intellect and intelligence are, I think and firmly believe, equally distributed among all races and peoples. Within those races, different sorts and kinds of talents are present. Sad to say, some races have attained greater economic power, have attained greater advantages, and have used this to appear smarter or cleverer than other racial groups. In short, most people can hardly be described as stupid in any respect, regardless of their race classification.

The Northern Caucasian races, until fairly recently, have dominated the scene. It must be said that the Mediterranean peoples, such as the Greek and Romans, and Egyptians, had at one time held power and sway. The scepter of power and culture was given over and handed to the peoples, that at that time were Barbarians, but eventually developed and rose up. This includes the present European nations such as the French, English, Russians, and Germans. At one time, the Chinese and Arab peoples were far in advance of the Europeans, especially at the time of the Middle Ages.

This discussion, however, has a focus. That focus is 1.) does race mean anything; and 2.) why do people use race as a club and a bludgeon over others. As I said, race is an accident of human development and is essentially meaningless. I am not a geneticist, a biologist, or an anthropologist, yet I have noticed, more on a practical basis, that as one proceeds farther south, the skin pigmentation becomes darker. This is true of Spanish people, Italian people, and Greek people. As one proceeds farther north, the skin pigmentation becomes remarkably lighter, such is true of the Scandinavians, Germans, and English. As one proceeds very far south the skin pigmentation becomes very dark, as is true in Africa. I can only speculate, since, as I said, I am not an anthropologist and I have no knowledge of the why and wherefore of such subject, that it appears that skin pigmentation, that is, the darkness of the skin, is probably an adaptation to the intense sun, that is to say a form of protection, or the result of extended contact with the sun, resulting in a darker skin.

In short, race means nothing. The question is, why does it appear to mean, in the world and society, a great deal? I think the answer is in human corruption and greed. Human beings twisted and bad as they are, will use anything to obtain power and dominance over others. If they can say the darker races are stupid, and so attain power over them and keep them at the bottom of society, they will do so. Race consciousness is connected with power and money. One race having the temporary power and money will essentially enslave or dominate the other race. For some reason or another, and I cannot account for this, the darker races have been subject to and victimized by this phenomenon.

This brings us to the concept and issue of class. Personally, I find class distinctions disgusting and abhorrent. No rational, sensible, intelligent, moral, and caring person can possibly believe, or even think to the slightest extent, that class matters. Again, class is a matter of who has the economic power at any given time. The persons having attained that power refer to themselves as the upper class. Those who lack power are referenced as the lower class. Unfortunately, these false distinctions have come to be connected with race. The lighter races have made a claim that they are somehow upper class, and having obtained dominance and economic power over the darker races, place them in the lower caste of society. This is a most common phenomenon. The white Arian invaders in India enslaved and made lower caste, the dark Dravidians. The English, French, Americans, and Spanish did the same to the Africans.

In sum, I not only object to race and class distinctions, but I can say they make me personally ill. Race and class distinctions are nothing more than phenomena of human corruption. It is a good thing to raise oneself and have a better education, more material goods, and more opportunities. Human beings, however, use their rise into the upper class to bludgeon and attack those below them. Again, human corruption and deficient human nature connect race with class. Race is good, since different kinds of people created differently, looking different, and having their own particular kinds and types of beauty and goodness, reveal God's creative plan and his revelation that he has love for all regardless of their color, the shape of their eyes, their height, their intelligence, or their wealth.

Race and class are good things. They are used, as usual, by lacking human beings corruptly and incorrectly, making a good world, a less good world, making a wonderful creation, where there is room for everyone, a blackened vision.

11. Universal Healthcare Now

In the United States, for some time, medicine and doctors have been connected with money. I think it is fair to say that doctors in the United States make a great deal of money, as do the drug manufacturers. How and why the health of a human being should be connected with the amount of their funds, and why doctors should be millionaires for the work they do is somewhat puzzling, in such an advanced western society, as is the case in the United States.

Personally, I do not happen to think 1) that someone's health and well-being should be connected with their economic caste or status, or 2.) that anyone should have to pay a lot of money and enrich the people who are committed to cure them. Doctors argue that they have long years of education, and possibly, in the case of surgeons, a shortened earning lifetime, and therefore they should make a lot of money. I do not think that follows. One undertakes to do something in life, whether building a house, creating and raising a family, or as I do, representing people in the solution of their legal difficulties, for the good of the task itself, and not necessarily to engage in personal self-enrichment and self-aggrandizement.

I hesitate to say this, but I have come to believe that when money becomes the sole object, corruption takes place and sets in. To me it is an outrage and disgrace that caring and curing should be connected with wealth, first, and second, that doctors should become wealthy because they render medical care and health.

In Europe, and in most other countries, medical care is basically subsidized and given to all, regardless of their funds or economic status. Mothers are given extended maternity leaves and given the opportunity to return to work.

The capitalist medical profession argues 1.) that there are emergency rooms to care for people who cannot afford medical care and 2.) that a private system provides better medical care than a socialized system. This is a run around and a fallacy, and nothing more than an excuse for continued self-enrichment on the part of the medical profession. Committed professional physicians, one hopes, will provide excellent and caring medical treatment, even though they may earn less money. If it is their criterion and choice to give good medical treatment only to those who pay them a lot of money, in my opinion, not only are they unfit as physicians, they are unfit as human beings.

Thus, I call in this essay, for universal healthcare. Health should not be a matter of money. The better medical care to all classes of society, the better chance we have for all persons to be enabled to grow, support their families, and contribute to society. Medicine, when it is made a matter of money, leaves people in the wayside, basically to die. Money-oriented medical care is uncaring and basically stupid. For every person who falls by the wayside and is not cared for because they lack funds, in a universal healthcare system they are raised up and we all are able, because they are raised up, to live in a better world. Universal healthcare makes a better world for us all. For every person who has the opportunity to have medical care there will be some person who will find a cure for cancer. That person who was excluded for lack of access to adequate medical care would not have the opportunity to find that cure for cancer, or write that great book.

I call for universal healthcare and socialized medicine because I do not buy into corrupt, twisted, money values that should be a matter of caring and concern for the health and well-being of each and every person.

12. The Religion of Former President Bush

Former President Bush lays claim to the Judeo-Christian faith and tradition in his public utterances. In support of this manifesto he says he is against Abortion, against Stem Cell Research, and against Homosexual Marriage. He seeks a Constitutional Amendment to bar the latter.

On these issues he may or may not present the Judaeo-Christian perspective since there is a division and variety of opinions in the Jewish or Christian communities on these issues. Evangelical Conservative Christians, Roman Catholics, and Greek Orthodox Catholics, I think, agree with the President on his particular stance on these issues, as well as Orthodox Jewry. Members of the Methodist,

Presbyterian, and Episcopalian, as well as Reformed Jewry, and members of the Congregational Church, may not agree with him. I believe the Christian perspective of former President Bush is a skewed, if not narrow and limited, religious vision. The Christian and Jewish faiths have as a vision one of charity and love. The Hebrew Bible and New Testament, whether in the Psalms or Gospels, command us to care for the poor, the underclass, the underprivileged, the sick, the infirm, the aged, and children. We are told in the Gospels that the poor are blessed and the humble will inherit the earth. We are told as well that it is more difficult for a camel to go through the eye of a needle than for a rich man to enter the kingdom of heaven. We are told we have to be like children and not like the rich man who ignores the plight of the needy beckoning at his door. The Psalms and the Prophets in the Hebrew Bible have a similar vision. The true Judaeo-Christian vision speaks not to exclude individuals based on their not adhering to a strict sexual morality, but to include what the world sees as the innocent, infirm, helpless, and powerless. Sexual Morality is only one narrow part of the whole moral picture and vision. To select Homosexuality or Women's Rights for particular condemnation and say that this is the Judaeo-Christian tradition is to be indifferent to the more significant social visions that these faiths embrace. The Judaeo-Christian tradition is much more than tittering about sexual misdeeds. It is not limited to condemning and ferreting out sexual infractions, telling women what they must do, and excluding homosexuals from the system. It is a vision of including; it does not embrace greed and does not seek alliance with the capitalist system, or any political system. The Judaeo-Christian moral vision is not constituted and defined by a series of edicts and condemnations all connected with sex. I suggest that former President Bush and all of us need to see the entire moral/religious Judaeo-Christian tradition as not a few narrow rules. It is ironic that the response of the New Testament to the condemnation of sexual morality when the people sought to stone the woman caught in adultery was an admonition to those individuals as to whether they themselves had sinned and a parting word to the woman for whom condemnation and destruction was sought to go and sin no more.

It is proven that oppression and power only last so long and can only keep the lid on so long.

Christians find power in the love of Christ and his sacrificial death for all humanity. I submit that love is a far greater power than any other kind of power. Other kinds of power are destructive, negative, and come to an end. The love of one another and the love of God and Christ creates, builds, and binds together. The love of God and Christ brings people into an uplifted community, not based on dominance, but based on equality and sharing. Perhaps it is ironic that the overwhelming cosmic love of Jesus Christ, Creator and Redeemer of Mankind, raises up the poorest of the poor, and those of little value to the world, who stand on their own as persons of great value in the eyes of the Ruler and Ultimate Judge of all men and women regardless of race, economic status, class, sex, or whoever, whatever, and wherever they may be. Their poverty and insignificance raises them to greatness in the eyes of Jesus Christ, who rules the world not by force or wealth, but by the power of his love. That love is the scandal of the Gospel, and unacceptable and a scandal to the world.

The power of love, I argue, is the greatest power that can or ever will be. Most people spend their whole lives trying to find people to like them, if not love them. They have scant success. When they do find that person, they are shocked and surprised. I posit the power of love is the greater power, and I note that for 2000 years, the Church of Christ, however mistaken at times, however incorrect at times, and however misdirected at times, has lasted and will outlast every empire and system built on oppression, hate, dominance, acquisitiveness, grabbing and getting.

13. Why We Need Unions

President Obama has lately infused many billions of dollars into Chrysler Corporation and General Motors to salvage them from possible bankruptcy and dissolution as viable companies. General Motors, in particular, claims that the pensions and salaries it pays its workers render it non-competitive with competing motor companies, particularly Japanese companies. In essence and sum, General Motors blames its financial woes on the bloated salaries and pensions of unionized workers.

The social and economic issue that arises is if unions render the pay scale and pension benefits so high that the company cannot compete in the market place, are unions therefore a bad thing and to be eliminated? I argue for unionization and the necessity for unions.

The union movement, which had its inception in the 1930s after a great struggle with management, brought the working class man and woman into the middle class. That was a good thing, since the stronger the middle class, the fewer people in poverty and struggling, the greater the viability of the social and economic system. But I argue for unions on a more basic thrust. Where one party has all the power, such as management, there is an abuse of power. Companies will pay the lowest pay scale they can, in our capitalist system, to get the most work out of their workers. That is not a good thing. Where one party has all the power, there is abuse, if not tyranny. It is an unfortunate fact and element of human nature that the party with absolute power may and will abuse it, even to the destruction of those over whom they have power.

In the workplace, and in the marketplace, there must be a balance of power. Workers do not individually have any power over their bosses and employers, except in our raw boned capitalist system, to choose to leave or stay. If they stay, they think it will benefit them, and if they leave, in our bare knuckled capitalist system, theoretically, they can better themselves. This system is too harsh. In reality, when management has the absolute say, workers are abused, used, and sometimes destroyed ultimately. Before labor unions there was child labor, work seven day a weeks, and ten hour days. Unions brought a balance of power to this unfair system.

In collective numbers there is strength. An analogy may be made to our democratic society. The reign on the power of our elected officials is the fact that they must be elected by the people; otherwise there would be a Hitler-esque tyranny. In the same way, collective unionization allows workers to obtain a fair wage and benefits to raise themselves up to a decent standard of living, whereby they may own houses, send their children to college, and, as I have said, enter the middle class. Without unions, we have a system of peonage, in which the working class population are virtual peonage labor with no hope of bettering themselves. Unions provide social stability; they provide a balance of power; and they provide a better life for the vast majority of people who are working class and who must work to survive. Unions bring the working class population from the edge of survival to a viable and decent standard of life and living. The General Motors workers bargained for pensions and a salary to support themselves and their families, not asking more than the ability to support their wives and children, pay their household mortgages, and have a decent retirement. This is good for us all. This is good for society. Unions are not merely good, but because of defective and corrupt human nature which given some power will likely abuse it, are desperately necessary.

14. Socialism and Capitalism: A Proposed Explanation and Answer

The two main economic systems in the world today are Socialism—to some extent Communism and Marxism—and Capitalism. Capitalism has come to dominate the economic scene in the world today. At one time, China and Russia were communist countries, but they have now switched to capitalist market systems. Western Europe, particularly Sweden, Denmark, Norway, Germany, Holland, Belgium, and to some extent France and England, have socialist systems, or at least, socialist/capitalist systems. These systems have pluses and minuses.

Capitalism, the argument goes, although based on greed and competition, gives many people a fighting chance, or rather a starting chance. The idea behind capitalism is that it provides opportunities for the creative, hard-working individual to succeed economically, or in whatever way he or she might wish.

Socialism and communism are based on the equalization and the equal distribution of wealth. The idea behind socialism is that the broad range of the population is provided with some sort of medical care, free education, and a job. Although, there are opportunities to economically outdo their neighbor, they are somewhat limited in their ability to attain whatever goal they might have in competition with their neighbor.

This little piece of literary work offers a solution as to why these systems both, in some sense, must inevitably and do fail on some level. For want of a better word, sin, human nature is corrupt and wanting. Therefore, in any system the most selfish, if not limited people in character, seek for domination and are disinclined to truly share the wealth and opportunities. The fault in these systems and reason why they fail is not in the systems, since the systems in some sense are good, especially socialism. The problem is that sinful, corrupt human nature engages in a power grab through the exclusion of others. Even in theoretically classless communism, a few individuals sought for and obtained power. The problem in these systems, sad to say and unfortunately, is not in the systems, but in ourselves, our weakness, our desire for power and wealth, and our disinclination to share. All systems must fail in some sense, not because the systems are bad, but unfortunately because people are bad.

One drop of Jesus' love can change a continent. What is not needed is better systems, but better people, spiritually giving and developed people, whose object is not self-aggrandizement, but charity and involvement with others in seeking not personal benefit, but benefits for all and a better world.

Notes

1. 497 US 261, 110 S. Ct. 2841, 111 L. Ed. 2d 224 (1990)
2. 52 NY 2d 363, 438 NYS 266 (1981)
3. 177 Misc. 2d 352, 675 NYS 807 (S. Ct., Queens County, 1998)
4. 273 AD 2d 929, 709 NYS 779 (4th Dept. 2000)
5. 75 NY 2d 218, 551 NYS 876, 551 N.E. 2d 77 (1990)
6. 162 Misc. 2d 697, 619 NYS 235 (S. Ct., Rockland County, 1994)
7. 155 Misc. 2d 103, 597 NYS 544 (S. Ct., New York County, 1991)
8. See on this also, *Delio v. Westchester County Medical Center*, 129 AD 2d 1, 516 NYS 677; Annotation, Judicial Power to Order Discontinuance of life-sustaining treatment by John D. Hodson, 48 ALR 4th 67, Lawyer's Co-operative Publishing Company, 1986.
9. The author is indebted in this research and in the cases cited here to Nancy Staar, a student in his paralegal class at Borough of Manhattan Community College whose brief on this subject, excellent in all respects, greatly contributed to the content and structure of this article.

Chapter 4
Literary and Philosophical Essays

Introduction

The next and final section of this book is a group of essays on literary and philosophical topics. The first essay is "On Words and Language" and analyzes the current disorder and sloppiness in word and language use in modern society. The essay "On Tradition" analyzes the pros and cons of traditions and concludes that some traditions are good and some are bad, just as some current fads or ideas may be good or bad, and, maintains that in both instances, we must analyze each concept or idea, whether founded under the rubric of tradition or currency, on an individual basis.

The essay "We Stand on their Shoulders" suggests that we stand on the shoulders of antiquity, and in particular, of the Graeco-Roman tradition and literature. The essay, "The Old are not to be Discarded," attacks the current idea of the youth culture and suggests that modern society could benefit from the wisdom and knowledge of the old and our senior citizens.

"On Relationships and Alienation," suggests, in our current impersonal electronic society, that relationships have become most difficult, and that, in our materialism we have become alienated from interpersonal loving contact and connection. The essay "Is Happiness Possible?" suggests that happiness is founded in relationships and in the apprehension of the world, on a daily basis, and all the goods it may chance to offer. The essay "What is Progress?" posits the idea that material progress is not necessarily intellectual, emotional, or spiritual progress.

The essay, "Moral Relativism or Absolute Truth" attacks the modern idea that there is no absolute truth and that values, ethics, and morality are purely relative. The final essay on "Power" concludes that the Christian ethic does not include a desire for power, but is founded on love, caring, and service by and for others.

1. On Words and Language

The English language, in America, now has long been tending to and has finally arrived at the stage of language at its earliest, if not primeval stage: monosyllabic and guttural syllables, not aiming to precise, narrative communication, nor to the highest form of poetic diction, but seeking to emulate the most intellectually vacant sectors of society: prostitutes, criminals, possibly long-shore men, and most certainly, television stars. In short, anyone who has anything to do with young persons between 14 and 30 is aware that four letter words of Anglo-Saxon derivation, once barred from polite conversation, have now become commonplaces of young and old, and those in between.

Placed between these expletives and vulgarities are "oh's" and "ok's." To speak, in America, in complete declarative sentences has become something of an anachronism, the province of the arts and academe. To speak in the language of Milton, Shakespeare, the Bible, and Bunyan is to appear, to many, as stuffy and attempting a sort of class superiority.

The English language, with its million word vocabulary, and with its rich admixture of Greek, Latinate, and Germanic elements, has become, if one can judge by everyday conversations of others at play and the workplace, not the prime, precise tool of the philosophy of Thomas Hobbes or the poetry and prose of the Authorized version of the Bible, but the language of the gutter, taking as its model, the behavior patterns, for want of a better description, of the lowest elements of society.

How can we account for this state of affairs and how can this development be explained?

Why has the lowest common denominator become the desideratum and norm?

There are three reasons. First, is egalitarianism. There is an unfortunate and underlying philosophical trend, both abroad and in the United States of America, that all men and women, whatever their attainments, whatever their accomplishments, and whatever their positions, are somehow intellectually, emotionally, and spiritually equal. It is true that, in the value of their souls and spirits before the Omniscient Creator, all men are in fact fully equal. Yet, this essential equality is not to be translated to the idea that J.D. Salinger and Saul Bellow, in the mode in which they express themselves, in their use of the English language, are equal to Shakespeare and Milton. Nor is Bertrand Russell, great though he is in the philosophical arena, to be regarded as equal to Plato. The notion of total equality, and all human beings' innate value before God, and their essential human equality, and their political equality as citizens of the greatest and most powerful constitutional democracy in the world, does not have as its logical corollary that the language of the lowest elements of society is desirable. This is an error.

In short, our positive desire to impose equality, democracy, and egalitarianism, is not to be translated into the idea that the lowest use of language, bowdlerized usage and now commonly used Anglo-Saxon epithets, are to be encouraged and imitated. In fact, in writing and speech, the clearest, precise, and most eloquent use of English, rather, is to be encouraged and imitated. Equality before the law and the Creator should not give rise and have as its corollary brutalizing the language that Shaw and Dickens so skillfully used.

The second reason for this error is the death and demise of the humanistic education. It used to be that the heritage of all educated men and women was the Classical Education, nothing more nor less than a thorough grounding in the Greek and Latin classics. Beginning with Caesar and Virgil in the Secondary School and continuing through Homer, Thucydides, the Greek Dramatists, Livy and Horace, the adolescent boy or girl not only was exposed to the great works of the classical languages, but compelled to render into English the difficult periodic sentences of Cicero and Thucydides, the poetry of Horace and the hexameters of Virgil and Homer.

Words and their beauty, like sharp swords that tear the heart asunder, were worn into the heart of the student. His or her spare time was reserved for the English classics, i.e., the English romantic poets such as Keats, Shelley, and Byron, and the greatest of English poets after Shakespeare, in this writer's opinion, Milton. By a subtle process of absorption and osmosis, respect for language and words was taken into the mind and soul of the reader. Let us remember, with few exceptions, that all of the greatest English poets, dramatists, and prose writers, such as Matthew Arnold or Hazlitt, were the products of this educational system. It was tough matter to chew, but produced many generations of writers, familiar with the great works of European literature, and provided these writers and thinkers with a fine ability to write and speak.

Sad to say, this humanistic education has, for some time, been under attack, a victim of multiculturalism and the new disciplines of business, science, and computer science. The college, as a vocational training ground, has put under attack the humanistic educational edifice that served our society for some thousands of years.

What we gain in one area, we lose in another. We may gain men and women proficient in the operation of word processors and able to get and do things faster and faster. This will not however enable them to write and speak in the fashion of the Sermons and Meditations of John Donne.

Finally, there is a third reason: that is the advent of alternative forms of communication. Once it was that written and, to a lesser extent, spoken words were the primary forms of scientific, literary, and polite communication. Now there are radio, network television, cable television, movies, DVDs, and computers that blare at us, to some degree, the basest forms of words and thoughts. Drama and movies have become, for some, the arena of pictorial frank animalism and the place of the basest language usage. It is thoughtful to recall that Aeschylus and Plato never felt it necessary to use a vulgarism in their language and writings as a vehicle for what we now know to be the highest expression of thought and beauty. Thus, we may say, that egalitarianism, the death of the humanistic educational system, and the new subjects such as computer science, the social sciences, and business, that have taken the place of humanistic training, and the development and necessity for non-written communication, have resulted in the demise of communication based on the written word. We now have a society of many fed on the image alone, and, as a result, impoverished in mind and spirit by *L.A. Law* and rock music. We have a society that, for the most part, can no longer speak, write, or think on the level that the greatest writers and thinkers in the past have taught us to see as possibilities. The precise use of language, written and spoken, has become lost in a sea of democratic egalitarianism, multiculturalism, and vocational training. It is food for thought that the great Victorian novels, now the subject of a small academic minority in the University and now the apparent sole province of academe, were once eagerly awaited in the next issue and installment of the popular magazine of their day. It is even more food for thought that the great western novels, now a challenge to the University student, rarely if ever read voluntarily, were once the leisure activity of Victorian ladies in their boudoirs taking second place to Belles Lettres, Poetry, and even theology and metaphysics.

The audience that once sat through a complex theological sermon, now has the attention span that can only listen to blaring lyrics of rock music in the tape decks of their automobiles as they proceed to work. Democracy is good and in fact all men are equal in the sight of God and of the law. Popular culture can be good and is good, and other subjects have rightly made their way and taken their place besides the humanities in the college and university curriculum.

Let us know and be aware, however, that when we move forward in one direction, we do not really go forward, but merely move in a different direction. What we gain in one sense, we lose in another. If we move forward in charity toward all and gain in other areas of knowledge, we lose in love and sensitivity for the beauty of words, language, and writing, that we may never have again. All the word processors and computers in the world will never replace or produce the 23rd Psalm indicted by a Hebrew poet three thousand years ago. Its beauty and continued ability to stir generation upon generation, whether in the original Hebrew or in the language of the Authorized Version, is a testament to what the human mind is capable of and can express in words and language, and cannot be replaced by the King of Rock and Roll or the ease, facility, and hurried writing that is so prevalent today.

2. On Tradition

When we speak of tradition and the traditional, young or old, we conjure up the staid, the set, and even the boring. We conjure up old men and women holding forth, at great length, on the good old days, when men were men, women were women, and everyone and all knew their place. The workplace was for men, and church and kitchen for women. In this mythical, traditional world, children respected their elders, Blacks knew their place, and all was right with the world.

This, however, is for want of a better world, a negative mythos and stereotype of what may be felt and meant by the words tradition and traditional. It is, in fact, a caricature of what, closely analyzed and thought through, may offer us much guidance and good things. The traditional and tradition are much more than stereotypes, i.e. traditional family, traditional roles, in short, behavior patterns fixed in stone by the alleged obfuscation, glue, and erroneous thinking from past centuries. In fact, tradition and the traditional should not be solely seen or meant as rejecting freedom of thought and freedom of action.

For tradition, the inherited thought and wisdom of many centuries of the Judaeo-Christian tradition, the way, or Tao, Oriental and Chinese thought, cannot be escaped, however much we may laud common law marriage, freedom of sexual action in any direction, and defy and criticize any purported authoritarian thought. Tradition has to do with the successful organization of society, implicitly, if not explicitly, handed down from one succeeding generation to another, given to generation upon generation, almost through a process of handed down osmotic thinking, behavior patterns, and forms of organization, developed, and given to us much, as a child, as it were, upon entering into the world, inherits and apprehends the love and devotion of his or her parents and siblings, throughout his or her life. Tradition is the inheritance, by trial and error, over many centuries, of what has come to be and is the success story. Tradition endorses the love and commitment of a man to his wife. Tradition is about the establishment of the love-relationship that nurtures and develops coming generation upon generation. Tradition, is about an inherited value system that speaks of respect for the elderly, love for little children, patriotism for the commonweal, and love for one's neighbors. Tradition seeks to control and avoid the chaos of human passion, self-interest, replacing these with, and instilling, forms and rules of behavior. Tradition chains rampant sexuality and passion to one wife and one woman.

Tradition, it is true, limits and barricades free love and free sexuality. In return, we gain the establishment of stable homes and families. Tradition narrows and channels the vagaries, if not outrages, of human behavior. In return, we gain civilization. For the free verse of Alan Ginsberg, we gain the Sonnets of Shakespeare and the epic poetry of Milton. For the commune, where all live free together, we gain the Gothic Cathedral.

Without tradition, and the traditional, we are left if not with utter and utmost chaos, than with a vacuum, with nothing but individual freedom of action left to fill the empty void. All thought, behavior, prose and poetry must, amid chaos and mass, be given form. You argue and may say, form is unnecessary and meaningless. It is to be true to oneself, the inner directive, that matters. We must discard forms to be true to ourselves. I say that courtesy and civilized behavior patterns preserve the feelings of others and I say that that is a good thing that we do not offend by saying what we like and do not like, like brutes and animals, that attack out of passion.

You say sex is the function of all animals. I say, men and women have feelings and that we express those feelings in our channeled sexuality. The result, is the traditional home and family, where our sexual passions are channeled and transformed into the family, the basic nurturing unit and foundation of society.

All art must be channeled into form from chaos. For every Jackson Pollack, there are Rubens, Rembrandts, and Da Vincis, all of whom worked within traditional forms, creating lasting and ultimate beauty. Tradition and the traditional in art, music, and writing, give meaning and direction to our behavior patterns or thinking, otherwise unchanneled and undirected. Unlimited and limitless personal freedom, at best, begets a cold and alienated individuality, and worst results in riot and chaos. Free thinking is no thinking. Free love is no love. Tradition, brings order to the primeval void and chaos of our feelings, passions, and thought processes.

How can I end this little essay? Perhaps, with a word of warning. Some traditions are good, and others are bad. Slavery was a basic function of American society until the mid 19th Century, probably justified by reasons of morality and tradition, and the alleged inferior minds and persons of Africans brought over here for that purpose. In fact, however, slavery had its basis and genesis in greed, the desire for money, and commercial interests. Slavery still obtains in some parts of the world. Slavery was wrong and that tradition was correctly eliminated. Women were perceived as properties until the late 19th Century, until they obtained their full legal rights independent of their husbands. That tradition, probably justified by an alleged order of society based on husbands and men as rulers, was also correctly modified and, as a result, society advanced.

In sum, some traditions are good and some are bad. The word "tradition" can be used as a justification for human malice and evil. Thus, all traditions, from generation to generation, as they grow, develop, and are discarded, must be closely examined to determine and understand their truth and validity. Perhaps the current fad for sexual freedom, which is a present tradition, will be examined and discarded at some future date for something else, and society advanced. All in all, it must be said that tradition insofar as we apprehend and take from it what is good, is good, and insofar as we discard what is bad, that discarding is the right thing to do.

I want to conclude this essay by saying many so-called traditions have stayed the test of time, whether they be the family, monogamy, marriage, heterosexuality, honoring your parents, or loving your neighbor. These are to be recommended and kept, having withstood the destructive forces that we as citizens, and our society as a whole, are continually assailed with.

3. We Stand on Their Shoulders

I am told now that children, in the first grade, are given computers to toll their sums and learn and compose their first and nascent paragraphs. Information is gained by computer, essays now composed on a word processor and entertainment obtained in the silence of the bedroom staying at one's computer. In a word, the printed word, as a means of entertaining one's self and informing is fast becoming a past relic. At one time men read the dramatic poetic monologues of Browning for pleasure; men and women read the novels of Charles Dickens, Henry James and George Eliot in magazine serial form. There was a time when men and women listened to the three hour sermons of John Donne and Lancelot Andrews and then read them. There was even a public for epic poetry—witness the publication in 1679 of Milton's *Paradise Lost.*

Reading tastes and habits have not only altered, but shifted to combine visual and oral mediums. If the printed book is not in danger of becoming extinct, it is surely in danger of being replaced by other more capturing and sensually exciting forms of oral and visual entertainment.

What then can we say of the relevance of Classical languages and literature, Greek and Latin; what reason can we offer for the study of long dead languages. The answer is much in every way. For better of for worse, we stand on the shoulders of the ancients, if not at their feet. Alfred North Whitehead offered the view that all Western philosophy was by way of being a footnote to Plato. Before the Christian or Muslim God, there was the unmoved mover of Aristotle, the first and primary cause above all other causes whereby the universal mechanism operates. St. Thomas Aquinas restates Aristotle in the light of revelation. Epic poetry, primarily in Homer and secondarily in Virgil, are the models of the genre. Virgil is the guide in Dante's *Divine Comedy* and *Paradise Lost* and the Italian epics of Tasso and Ariosto find their source in Virgil.

Whether it is epic or the choral lyric of Pindar, Greek Tragedy or Roman Comedy, we of the West owe almost every poetic and dramatic form to the Greeks and Romans. Before Bacon, Montaigne, or Ralph Waldo Emerson there were the essays of Cicero on Friendship and on Moral Duties. The romantic novel of today has its source and is a lineal descendant in the ancient novel of Apuleius.

There is nothing new under the sun. Our so-called modern ideas find their source in ancient philosophy. Feminism is the new wave of the millennium. Plato, in the Fifth Book of the Republic, posited the equality of women and argued for their equality in the educational, governmental and social spheres. Communism finds its ultimate model in Plato's ideal state where philosophers are kings.

If we are not to be victims of our continued mistakes, sin and ignorance, or if we are not to limit ourselves to current fads and our own particular parochial schools of thought, and if we are perchance to step outside of our own limited sphere for a day, the Classics remain relevant and telling.

The Greeks and Romans still speak to us, in our time, in their literature and art, expressing ultimate beauty, form and original thought. We have not grown beyond them or away from them, but remain their children, growing in our minds and persons as any child does, but ever knowing and mindful that whatever is ideal, spiritual, metaphysical and literary in ourselves will never be severed from them. You who have gone beyond the whims of youth know full well the approach to the gates of death and the tie that binds us to them. For as we die we cease to fight those who have given us life.

The past still speaks to us, dead or alive, advising, loving and pointing the way out of our limitations to our continued relationship with the past.

We do a disservice to our children when we leave them in the ignorance and abyss of the current modern novel, the daily newspaper, and the computer. To think one is modern because one is in the throes of some current idea, be it feminism, Marxism, or materialism, is to be cut off and benighted.

The classics free us of our modernity, free us of our presumptions and desire for a relevance found first in the Dialogues of Plato. To know the Classics is to be a little more liberated from oneself, a little freer and somewhat more human than thought possible. We reject them at our peril.

4. *The Old Are Not to Be Discarded*

We live in a time where youth is worshipped. Those who choose to view sitcoms in the evening or soap operas in the afternoon on the networks rarely, if ever, see a man or woman under thirty. All are, or seem to be, laughing, joking, and frolicking, personifying the would be desideratum of the teenager who has and will never grow to maturity and old age. Whether it be the superman of *L.A. Law*, or the troublesome amours of *The Edge of the Night*, American Society, through it all, is devoted to the La De La Maiden and the Macho Young man. The Old on the media and stage are, if not discarded or even invisible, then the butt of humor, out of it and not with it, offering no knowledge or wisdom, for the most part leaning on their slightly occasional comic parental role.

It is the scandal of private industry that no one under fifty is permitted to serve. The "Golden Door" of "early" retirement is, if not pressured, then gently forced on the middle-aged worker to the point of termination, and firing.

True life, as we know it, is most surely a continuum. The child, adolescent, or young adult just graduated from the University and about to embark on the journey of life, is the tabula rasa, filled with some few facts, often sadly, solely connected with the computer operation, but bereft of the experience in life and letters that fully forms and informs the mature mind. As we grow old, though our bodily machine may come to wear, our minds and souls and hearts grow up and away, beyond the naiveté of youth.

In short, the true intellect is finally formed and continues to flourish beyond academic content knowledge as life continues, sifting and absorbing the increasing knowledge and wisdom that life offers us all.

In the journey we call life, through youth, middle age, and finally old age itself, we grow and develop and dream and create further and more completely. Though our bodies decay, our souls expand, not merely in ourselves, but beyond the egotism of youth to the interconnection and interdependence of age.

Other societies fail to share our fear and aversion of old age, but see the old as a resource, a repository of wisdom, knowledge, and experience.

The Mediterranean societies of Italy and Greece link the old with the young and middle-aged in three-tiered households, so allowing the three generation, to learn and absorb from the other; the Chinese do likewise.

It is the way of civilized man not to reject the old, not to warehouse them lest they be seen to offend us by their physical slowness and disability, but to honor and respect them.

It is only the very young, in their colossal egotism that know all and see all. It is the old, in their compassion and tolerance, that know how little they know and how much they have yet to understand.

Verdi wrote his greatest operas in his old age. Milton wrote his greatest narrative poems and play, *Paradise Lost, Paradise Regained,* and *Samson Agonistes,* in his blindness and infirmity.

Thomas Hobbes, one of the greatest English philosophers, began his career with a translation of Thucydides from the Greek. He ended it with a translation of Homer's Odyssey at the age of ninety. Kant produce his greatest philosophic treatises after the age of fifty. The Bible teaches us to honor the widows.

. To reject the continuum of life is not only to reject fully developed thought and art, stemming from a melding of education, art, and experience that is the success of age, but to reject the reality of life itself. For, true to say, at whatever stage of life we be, we are on a continued journey. No one would wish to be eternally young, limited in our outlook to reveling on the beach in bikinis and briefs, playing radios that speak only of young love and not compassion and charity. We all face the prospect, not to be feared or derided but cherished, of going beyond the emptiness of youth, to the wisdom, calm, and love of old age.

It is the way of life that though our bodies wither with the ravage of time, our hearts, souls, and minds continue to grow, knowing ourselves more fully and knowing others more completely.

Each day we stand at the gates of death itself. In that sense we are all old with each passing day, growing not to be slow and dull, but attaining to relationship with the reins of life itself, growing more fully and human and humane.

For what makes us fully human, is not the youth, our chests, or our breasts but our continuing capacity to grow in intimacy and interrelationship.

To reject the old is to reject the truth of life itself; it is to reject to what finally and completely makes us human, beyond erotic love and success, to the intertwining of ourselves with each other and ultimately with the Creator.

5. *On Relationships and Alienation*

We see the personal ads in daily newspapers and in magazines such as *The New Yorker*—boy wishes to meet girl. It seems, beyond the sought for romance, the long walks in the woods, and the still burning fires, is the desire possibly for raw sex or, more probably, for connection, in short, for some little human companionship.

The sexual revolution it seems, spelled the end of lifetime marriage in which, to be sure, many possibly suffered and from which many wanted to escape an unhappy and locked-in sterile relationship, where divorce, not then easily available, had to be obtained in such far away countries as Haiti, the Dominican Republic, or Mexico. The sexual revolution in the 1960s brought an end to long formal engagements and courtships and elaborate weddings, bringing in its wake a facile total equality and equity, bringing with it, rather than the cloak of Sir Walter Raleigh, the single-parent family. The world of *Leave It to Beaver* or *Father Knows Best*, sitcoms presenting the mythos of the American family, have been left behind for bisexual couples, lesbian parents, and Woody Allen and his lover Mia Farrow.

It was thought that this freedom, unleashed in the 1960s, would bring millennial happiness. Yet, it seems that it has brought in its wake a kind of loneliness and spiritual vacuum, despite the depictions in the popular magazines and television images. In truth, human beings seek nothing more than simple friendship and a little companionship to assuage our, it would seem, alienation and isolation. Why has this freedom that we thought would bring in the millennium brought in only isolation, loneliness, and alienation? Why, when we are no longer locked in to traditional marriage and family, our former one choice of life structure, do we exchange it for lack of connection and isolation? Why are there images in newspapers and popular magazines in the land, lauding the goal and benefit of total freedom, when people advertise for simple friendship? Why has this freedom, so vaunted and desirable, brought in only a vacuum, rather than personal fulfillment? Why in this era of multiple choices and options do human beings need to advertise for a little simple companionship and friendship?

Possibly the answer is in the present narcissism or devotion to self, which emphasizes getting as much for yourself and doing as much for yourself as you can, which has brought, it would seem, nothing more than spiritual emptiness and inner desolation and destruction. Why when we can fulfill every desire, do we only desire, and cannot obtain, simple human connection?

In fact, we need institutions, whether they be church, synagogue, family or the state. As human beings we need institutional direction. As persons we need standards and uplifting behavior patterns. Unlimited personal freedom and self-love apparently bring nothing but vacuity.

We are all ultimately entwined and interconnected with one another. From the dinners on our tables, the food products, the farmers, and the grocers, each of us need one another.

Denying our interconnection in the name of personal freedom and doing what you want, brings only loneliness and being cut off. It is significant that the 20th Century, with all its emphasis on fulfillment and freedom has produced no great romantic love poet. Total freedom is total sterility. Institutional behavior patterns or, as it were, a mixture of the personal and institutional, curb our desires and self-love and self-adulation and directs us to proper love-founded relationships. True freedom lies in living our lives in connection and relationships with others as we move through the course of our lives. Unlimited freedom brings nothing but spiritual death.

It is only connection and relationship with one another, founded in the course and stream of our lives, that bring any happiness. It is only in devotion and service to others that we can know the way to happiness. Hell, if it exists, must be founded in egotistical self-love and only brings spiritual and emotional death. We only find ourselves when we lose ourselves.

It is sad, but true, that many seek through newspaper and magazine advertisements, a kind of personal fulfillment that can only be obtained and conquered by losing ourselves in others. Ultimate freedom can only be found in interconnection, rather than in the highly individualistic capitalist society in which we all are forced to function. The answer is not in ourselves, but in those that surround us. In sum, the single minded devotion to self brings in its wake, deeply felt unhappiness. It is only in institutions and others that bind us and do not pull us apart, that we can become fully human.

6. Is Happiness Possible?

All of us, men and women, want happiness. For some, if not many, in the modern world, the chosen route to happiness consists of the further and greater acquisition of wealth and material goods. For those who, for want of a better word, adopt materialism as their philosophical guidepost and benchmark, happiness is found in more and more money, and more and more goods. Others seek happiness in sex and sexuality. These are the modern Epicureans, who in continued sexual and sensual pleasure hope to find happiness. Others seek happiness in culture and the life of the mind, whether literature, music, art, or philosophy, in a word, intellectual activity. This group, in our world of today, are a somewhat thinner group than used to be, since materialism has displaced literature, the humanities, and philosophy as the prime end and force of the societal mechanism.

Given these many options, one might ask, in what does happiness consists and how may it be had and obtained? I suggest five ingredients essential to a happy life.

The first ingredient to happiness, I think, and of a happy life, is the community and affection that can only be obtained within the traditional family. A fulfilling and happy family life is a basic ingredient of the happy life. It is only in the family structure of wife, husband, and children, that there can be that community and exchange of love and affection that largely makes life tolerable.

The second ingredient of happiness, I believe, is fulfilling work. For many, if not all, work consists largely of sameness and drudgery. For most, work is routine, boring, or physical in character. Thus, for the factory worker, or clerk in a store, retirement as early as possible is a welcome relief.

Work which is intellectually challenging and fulfilling, but which involves the solution of human difficulties and problems, can add a great measure of happiness to the life of any man or woman.

In short, work which may enable one to make some sort of positive contribution to society can significantly add to the happy life.

The third and, perhaps, very essential ingredient for happiness is some measure of good health. For those of us who spend and live our life in constant pain and suffering, life is burdensome and difficult. It is fair to say that without some degree and measure of health, life is, and becomes, largely intolerable. Good health increases our chances for some sort and degree of happiness.

The fourth and, perhaps, the most general basis for happiness, and the happy life, is the ability to go outside of ourselves, our egos, and our narcissism, and involve ourselves in the lives of others.

It is only by stepping outside of ourselves and touching the hearts and minds of others, if not loving and serving them, that a measure of happiness may be had. Many, if not most of us, spend the large measure of our lives in some sort of constant self-involvement. We largely wallow, throughout our lives, in self-love. In this, misery must consist, since self-love and intense self-involvement lead to nothing more than ennui, boredom, and, in the end, gross unhappiness. It is only by stepping outside ourselves and involving ourselves in the joys, affections, sorrows, and pains of others that some fulfillment, if not happiness, becomes possible.

How then can happiness be had?

For the happy man and woman the world is a place of infinite possibilities and treasures. The contented, if not happy, man and woman, as they go through life, involve themselves mightily and completely with what life may happen to offer to them. The happy man and woman takes from day to day, and from year to year, what life may offer them, always seeking involvement, in love and affection, with their fellow human beings. The happy man and woman grasp the goods of life as they come to him or her, always seeing, in every circumstance, situation, and person, endless possibilities and endless potentialities for interest, affection, and involvement.

The happy man and woman go through life with zest, taking what may be before them, or may be offered to them, declining none, and embracing all, seeing in every person, creature, rock, flower, or stone, the variety and infinitude of the creator and the creation, seeing in everyone the chance and opportunity for involvement, that by taking the person outside of himself or herself, offers the only chance for happiness.

Finally, I think, there is a fifth ingredient for happiness, which is a sense of the transcendent. The happy man or woman, I think, sees potential and possibilities beyond his or her immediate material environment. The happy man and woman has a feeling and sense of the transcendent and spiritual that, on some level and basis, gives him or her a sense of joy and connection with what is beyond himself or herself, and gives him or her a feeling that every man and woman will be in community with Him or her in spirit. Thus, the happy man and woman sees value and importance in every man, woman, or child, whatever their race, class, or sexuality, knowing that in their connection with him in spirit he will be with them and beyond them.

7. What Is Progress?

In our present age and society, it would appear that we are in the midst and throes of great progress. This progress seems to take many forms and so can and may be defined in a number of ways. To begin with, in medicine, with the advent of anesthesia, antibiotics, and advanced surgery we have greatly extended the human life span and made life for most persons easier and more fulfilling. There are many cures for formerly incurable diseases that in former days ended life completely. Thus, many diseases such as Tuberculosis, Polio, and Measles have been completely eliminated. Advances in medicine, thus, have brought about an extended lifespan and a more pain free life for most of us.

In similar fashion there has been great progress in technology. With the advent of computers and technology in general, life has been speeded up and everything and anything has become more accessible. The distance has been eliminated, to a large degree, and connection between persons, if not nations, is more rapid, speedier, and easier. The result has been globalization and the virtual elimination of national, religious, and racial distinctions. Machinery and technology have made life more facile and with email communication we may reach out and touch whomsoever and wherever we will. With more rapid communication in transportation we are in striking distance of anyone or anywhere on Earth.

In these areas progress has occurred, and it can be confidently said that life is better for most of humanity who can avail themselves of these advances. In other areas, technology and medicine have accomplished little, if anything. We are still spiritual and poverty-stricken moral cripples. The 20th Century has witnessed massive human slaughter in two World Wars, as well as a number of genocides including the Armenian genocide committed by the Turks; the Jewish genocide; the genocide of Pol Pot; the Rwandan genocide; the genocide in former Yugoslavia; and most recently the genocide occurring in Darfur in the Sudan. The massive slaughter that followed the Russian Revolution should not be left unmentioned. We still kill, maim, and torture our fellow human beings. We attack our spouses, verbally, and sometimes physically. Fathers decline to support their children and mothers, at times, choose not to bother with them, or abort them in the first place.

We have made materialism and narcissism our benchmark and desideratum. The advances in technology and medicine have not been matched by our puny, if not non-existent, personal, moral, and ethical progress. If not for laws that controlled human behavior, life would be impossible and intolerable.

Our souls are dry rot. We are served with a diet of meaningless poverty-stricken concepts and ideas generated by television and the internet. We invent more and more sophisticated weapons of mass destruction to kill more and more people, and technology and machinery have been employed to effectively kill more people more efficiently.

There has been some moral and ethical progress, at least in the Western world, since we no longer torture people in the stocks, employ the whipping post, boil them in oil, drown them, or burn them at the stake as occurred well into the 19th Century. We still employ the death penalty, rather than incarcerate someone, which costs too much and offers the chance for rehabilitation and change for that person. In short, we have grown away, if not from, drawing and quartering people.

On the other hand, there has been little progress in literature, for example. Poetry, once a popular art form, is now the province of specialized academics. We have no Dantes, Miltons, Virgils, Keats, Shelleys, or Victor Hugos. We produce massive glass structures, notable for their size alone, but cannot produce a gothic cathedral dedicated to the glory of God. In short, we produce cars, pedestrian malls, and buildings of massive ugliness and monstrosity.

With progress comes decline. What we gain in one sense, we lose in others. We can only say that we are still moral and ethical barbarians and employ technology to kill and maim, employing medicine to treat the maimed and crippled.

We may eliminate distance, do things faster, and live longer, but we still on a continuous and intense basis inflict pain and suffering on our fellow human beings, and having done so remain largely indifferent to the pain and suffering we may have inflicted.

Whether progress has occurred and has happened at all remains a question.

8. *Moral Relativism or Absolute Truth*

Moral relativism, so called, has gained in the United States and many Western nations and societies, currency, if not widespread acceptance. The idea behind moral relativism is that there are no set or absolute moral or ethical rules and, as a result, it follows there is no absolute truth or truths. Moral choice is apprehended not as an absolute, but, as an individual choice, from person to person, and from age to age.

Thus, for example, adultery, once codified as a crime, has subsequently come to carry nothing more than a severe societal stigma. Adultery has now gained a degree of tolerance, if not outright acceptance.

Casual sexual liaisons, also, conducted outside of the marriage bond, once stigmatized, have gained widespread societal acceptance.

Consensual homosexual relations, once known as consensual sodomy, also in the past regarded and codified as illegal have, as well, gained toleration.

At this point in time in most Western societies we do not tolerate, and have stopped short of tolerating and accepting, incest or adult/child sex, but appear to be moving toward total acceptance of same-sex or homosexual marriage.

Moral relativism, as an idea, implies if not states that "you can do what you want" and gain toleration, if not approval, as long as you harm no one outright, and break no laws.

Absolute truth posits there are fixed ethical and moral norms, the deviation from which constitutes some sort of wrongdoing or moral error, which should not be tolerated or accepted and which deserve to be stigmatized, if not made illegal and punished.

Moral relativism has its roots in a number of misleading and erroneous thought sources. The moral relativist says that as long as what you do in some sense makes you feel good and does not constitute a bother or irritation to anyone in your vicinity, it is seen as ok. This idea has its source in the media, where television, computers, and, of course, the Internet present deviate and illicit sexual behavior as fine and implicitly, if not explicitly, encourage it. A glance at Internet chat rooms and personal advertisements shows this to be true, as well as the widespread dissemination of pornographic material at all newsstands and places we can buy things.

The media, as a source of moral and ethical truth is, charitably put, faintly, if not actually, ridiculous, since the promotion of these purported lifestyles and images has its source in the desire of its purveyors to obtain for themselves wealth and financial gain. This desire to make money, as a source of these ideas, constitutes a kind of corruption with the result that what the media presents as the image and desideratum of what we as men and women should do and be, is nothing more than an outright bald-faced lie, emanating from the desire for personal enrichment on the part of its creators and purveyors.

The second source of error in the concept and principle of moral relativism is a misinterpretation, or rather misapprehension, of what is meant by democracy.

In a democracy there is a belief that all men's and women's opinions have equal value and validity in the free and open market place of ideas that constitutes a free society. In sum, we are led to believe that since everyone has an equal vote, that therefore what they may happen to say constitutes some sort of truth. This is a misconstruction and misinterpretation, I think, of democracy. What everyone happens to say does not have equal intellectual validity or truth, and should not, therefore, be given equal credence. The idea that this should be so stems from the mistaken idea that all men and women are actually equal in their talents, intelligence, and ability.

A democracy is nothing more than a system of political equality, giving all its citizens an equal voice in the electoral process and voting franchise. Rich and poor, intellectual and worker, disabled and healthy, are all given an equal role in the governing process, insofar as they all have the same vote.

Let me add that democracy is the best of all systems, since it distributes power among all its citizens, with the result that any tendency on the part of one or more individuals to obtaining absolute power is checked and limited. Democracy, however, does not mean that all of us are equal. I may be a good lawyer, but I will never be a professional tennis player, a concert pianist, or even a rock star.

It follows from this that not all opinions and ideas should be given the same toleration and given the same sort of respect. Thus, this misinterpretation of democracy, which is nothing more than a political system, leads to the mistaken view that morality is solely an individual matter and has no reference to any form of absolute truth.

The third source of the error of moral relativism is what has come to be called "political correctness."

We, all of us, want to fit in and not publicly oppose what I hesitate, but must call, the current propaganda and jargon that is constantly and continuously inflicted on us all. We fall in with whatever, as it were, is in the air. All of us know that greed and the worship of material goods and money as a final end is not only wrong, but absurd.

Political correctness forces us publicly to say otherwise.

What then can we say? Is it better to apprehend truth on the basis of what each person regards as personally appropriate for their particular situation or put it another way, what the particular age or Zeitgeist recommends at any particular time.

I admit that so-called fixed moral rules can and do lead to great human suffering if they are not carefully examined from age to age and from generation to generation.

Since human beings and human nature are in some sense corrupt, that corruption will operate in the name of a fixed morality to bring about and create wrong and moral errors, such as slavery, the oppression of women, or any other form of injustice. Corrupt human beings and their leaders will use morality and moral rules for whatever corrupt political purpose they may have, whether to gain power for themselves over less powerful and unfavored groups, or simply to get more money.

Withal I believe that moral relativism as a thought base and idea system is incorrect. Its sources—the media, greed, and misleading political thinking—mean that, as an idea, it has little or no value. Political correctness, the forces of greed, and corrupt political leadership say to us that adultery and casual sexual liaisons are perfectly fine. We all know within our hearts and spirits that they are not. The media says through bombarding us with pornographic images that that is ok. We all know within our hearts it is not. We all know that the single-minded desire for material goods and wealth as a value system is totally bereft of any intellectual validity. We are told by our corporate and political leaders that this should be our lodestar.

In short, we, within our deepest levels of consciousness as human beings, do believe that there are absolute moral norms and absolute truth. We call this natural law, for want of a better word. We all agree that we should be nice to the people around us. Christianity tells us to love our neighbor. In some sense, there is a universal thought system of moral law that informs and permeates our entire society. I am not convinced that what is purveyed by the media, what is in the air, or what is mistaken as tolerance constitutes any sort of truth. Some things are true, and others are not. I am not prepared to have the source of my thinking and life principles, molded by whatever happens to be faddish or fashionable, imposed on me and all of us for reasons of personal financial gain on the part of its makers, who inflict these corrupt ideas on us, solely for the purpose of attaining power.

9. Power

For many men and women, power is the desideratum and end goal of life. Generally, people hope to gain power through the acquisition of material wealth or through their job or position. People want power, I think, for two reasons. First, and this is a rather defective and twisted reason, is to obtain control, if not oppression, over others. This control and oppression can occur in a job, where one has been invested with some power and control over others "below him" in rank,, position, or role. The power can be that of a Judge, the power of a CEO, or the more limited power of a middle-manager or bureaucrat.

Be that as it may, many people want this control and might over others. This desire for power is imbedded in human nature and is connected with finding a way or method of raising oneself upon the "common herd." I believe this desire for power is basically human weakness.

People want power for another reason. The powerless are victimized. Those who acquire sufficient power are shielded from the oppressions of those that might use their power against their powerless estate. People seek power because they are protected from attack, undermining, jealousy, and vicious assault on the part of their competitive neighbors.

The Christian, or rather the Christian ethic, does not include the desire for power and its attainment. Christians desire to serve others and to contribute to society in a positive way. Christians, however, have another kind of power and a far greater power. All power in the commonly understood sense of the word comes to an end. Oppressive communism had a short-lived life; fascism in the persons of Mussolini and Hitler came to an end in fifteen years. Oppression only works so long. Imperialism had to give way to independence. It is proven that oppression and power only last so long and can only keep the lid on so long.

Christians find power in the love of Christ and his sacrificial death for all humanity. I submit that love is a far greater power than any other kind of power. Other kinds of power are destructive, negative, and come to an end. The love of one another and the love of God and Christ creates, builds, and binds together. The love of God and Christ brings people into an uplifted community, not based on dominance, but based on equality and sharing. Perhaps it is ironic, the over-whelming cosmic love of Jesus Christ, Creator and Redeemer of Mankind, raises up the poorest of the poor, and those of little value to the world, who stand on their own, as persons of great value in the eyes of the Ruler and Ultimate Judge of all men and women regardless of race, economic status, class, sex, or whoever, whatever, and wherever they may be. Their poverty and insignificance raise them to greatness in the eyes of Jesus Christ, who rules the world not by force or wealth, but by the power of his love. That love is the scandal of the Gospel, and unacceptable and a scandal to the world.

The power of love, I argue, is the greatest power that can or ever will be. Most people spend their whole lives trying to find people to like them, if not love them. They have scant success. When they do find that person, they are shocked and surprised. I posit the power of love is the greater power, and I note that for 2000 years, the Church of Christ, however mistaken at times, however incorrect at times, and however misdirected at times, has lasted and will outlast every empire and system built on oppression, hate, dominance, acquisitiveness, grabbing and getting.

10. A Few Words about Feelings

All of us are concerned about feelings, mainly our own. Sad to say, we give little thought to other people and their feelings, and as I said, we are rather egre-giously and absolutely concerned with our own, typical of human self-involvement and egotism. This little essay will concern itself with analyzing feelings.

The first thing that must be said is that feelings are very inexact indicators of truth. Our feelings may be affected when someone chooses not to talk to us, or declines, or is indifferent to that issue. In reality, that person may be simply living their life without reference to our feelings at all, or to ourselves at all. We interpret their indifference or lack of attention to us as a stab at our feelings and personhood. At times, our feelings are affected when someone speaks to us in what we perceive as an overly harsh, cutting, and mean spirited fashion. That may be the way that person speaks to everyone, and that particular behavior pat-tern is not directed to us or our feelings.

Thus, as we see by these examples, our feelings interpret things and twist them, misleading us and, so, are not very exact indicators of truth. Second, in the present state of society, feelings do not occupy a very great role. An example would be the ideal of romantic love, which governed western culture for some 1900 years, up to the present time, when lust has taken over. If we chance to view the movies or listen to the Broadway shows of the 1930s and 1940s we see romantic love featured. Men and women approach each other gingerly, and barely touch. At that time, in society, love was paramount, not lust. The films of that era depicted men and women as falling in love and getting married. The films of today portray them as jumping into bed—to wit—the James Bond films. The popular music of our day is crude and its lyrics, at times, offensive, featuring animal passion, as opposed to the love song of *South Pacific,* one of the great Broadway shows of the 1940s, "Some Enchanted Evening." If we have not grown up from love, I think we have grown away from it, and so, feelings are nulled and hidden, and not really featured. The delicacy of romantic love and the love songs of the Broadway stage have been overcome by crude, loud, blaring cacophony, featuring grotesquely offensive lyrics.

One may speculate that the reason for this is the decline of the Christian worldview, which encouraged and promoted love leading to marriage. That worldview has been slowly eroded, and in some cases eliminated, depending on whom you are talking to.

A final point in this little literary byway about feelings. Feelings and emotions differ between the child and the adult. The child is concerned, if not twisted and obsessed, with his own feelings and being loved, or better put, being the recipient of love from his parents, teachers, and other adults that he or she looks up to. Adult feelings are different. Compassion, kindness, and charity are adult emotions and feelings. They concern themselves not with the feelings of our person in our self, but concern, consideration, and humanity as respects others. Only a mature adult can realize and express these feelings.

What then can we say of feelings? What with cell phones, emails, computers, ipods, dvds, and television and movies, feelings and relationships are distant and removed, and so love is distant and removed. This is another reason why feelings are on the decline in our present society. We are more and more separated by technology and electronics, and the opportunity to form giving, concerned, compassionate, humanitarian relationships is becoming and has become more and more difficult if not unreachable.

One may hope that human relationships will make a comeback from the forces of darkness that assault us men and women. A world without feelings met between persons is a gray, boring world, unforgiving, and without growth and dynamism. One may hope that there will be a return to the romantic and humanitarian ideal, which is the only way to true growth.

Index

Breinigsville, PA USA
30 November 2010

250368BV00002B/4/P